How I cook

Quadrille
PUBLISHING

Skye Gyngell

How I cook

PHOTOGRAPHY BY
Jason Lowe

Notes • Please use sea salt, freshly ground pepper and fresh herbs. • Choose organic free-range eggs. Anyone who is pregnant or in a vulnerable health group should avoid recipes using raw egg whites or lightly cooked eggs. • Buy unwaxed citrus fruit if possible, especially if you are using the zest. • Timings are for fan-assisted ovens. If you are using a conventional oven, turn the setting up by 10–15°C (1 Gas mark). Use an oven thermometer to keep a check on the temperature.

Introduction

I thrive on the stimulation I get from running a restaurant – working with a team of talented chefs and creating new dishes inspired by the wonderful seasonal produce available to us right through the year – but I can honestly say that the greatest pleasure I derive from food is cooking for loved ones. Bringing friends and family together around a table at home to enjoy food, share conversation and relax together is deeply satisfying. Entertaining needn't be demanding or time-consuming. At home, I like to keep food and cooking simple. It's easier on the shopping and gives me more time to spend with my family – and guests when I'm entertaining. I wanted to share the food I cook at home with you, not least because I am aware that so many of us are time-pressured these days and I was keen to offer some solutions in the kitchen. However busy we are, it's important to make time to enjoy ourselves. And, for me, the pleasure of cooking for others – of witnessing their enjoyment of my food – is second to none. Above all, that's what this book is about: delighting others through food – with ease, generosity, unpretentiousness, and a little finesse...

However small your garden, even if you have nothing at all – just room for a little window box – I encourage you to grow some herbs. Fragrant top note herbs, such as basil, parsley and soft thyme, inspire me in the kitchen and remind me of sunshine.

Essentially, this is a collection of the recipes that I cook at home, arranged by the kind of meal – from breakfast through lunch and tea to evening meals and late-night suppers – encompassing everyday dishes as well as special occasion food. Within the chapters, the recipes are arranged as a series of menus, though these are merely my thoughts and ideas for putting together dishes that complement each other comfortably and respect the seasons; they are not in any way set in stone. As ever, my cooking is strongly inspired by the produce in season and I always seek to bring together ingredients that appear at the same time; so often they have a natural affinity. You can, of course, mix and match menus at will, or simply pick recipes to cook at random. There are absolutely no rules.

Along the way, I have given simple tips and offered some specific advice on cookery skills. My cooking is not defined by complex techniques, because I prefer to keep things easy, but over the years I have come to realise the importance of mastering a few basics. It really isn't difficult to make your own crisp, light pastry, whisk egg whites to the peak of perfection, fold flour delicately into a sponge mixture, or cook a velvety smooth custard without it curdling... once you know how. I've also tried to take some of the mystery out of cooking methods, such as slow-cooking, roasting and pan-frying. Like most things in life, these simple skills are down to practice – knowledge brings confidence and repetition breeds understanding.

People often say to me it's alright for you, cooking and entertaining isn't demanding for you. It is my job, of course, and I am fortunate enough to do it all day, every day. In truth, it is something I feel comfortable with, but there are so many areas of my life in which I don't feel as self-assured. Slowly I am learning that if I practice things I feel overwhelmed by, they become easier to accomplish and my confidence grows. It is the same with cooking. So just start and don't worry about making mistakes for they are learning curves. Embrace the spirit of why you are doing it, and – above all – enjoy yourself. Hopefully you will find, as I do, that it is incredibly satisfying. I cook for the same reason that you do – to bring joy to others – it pleases me to see people smile and laugh and feel content around a table, and I'm sure it is the same for you.

In many ways cooking is now more confusing than ever, owing to the tidal wave of information about food, its provenance, seasonality and availability. We are perplexed by questions, such as is it fair trade, organic, sustainable? When confronted with so many considerations, it can be difficult to decide what to cook. And when we are entertaining, we need to choose a menu that will suit everyone. One way of sidestepping these issues is to design a menu that revolves around practicality. Ask yourself, will this menu suit the number of guests, the time you have available to prepare it, and the time of year? Above all, simplify things... perhaps adding a little touch of extravagance.

Food often requires more in the way of concentration than skill, so try to give it the attention it deserves. Rushed, distracted cooking is often reflected in its final taste.

A feast should be just that – abundant and with a great spirit of generosity – not necessarily in terms of quantity, but in terms of thought. The taste, smell and sight of food make for memories. Now, well into adulthood, I have fond recollections of Easter egg hunts and the tastes of the eggs that we ate with gusto upon discovering them. And of Christmas in the sweltering heat at my grandmother's house, where we ate the same things year after year: tinned asparagus laid neatly on to plates, cold turkey and potato salad, followed by a steaming pudding with sixpences hidden inside. It wasn't the best food in the world by any means, but it's the stuff of memories. And for me now, the most important part of cooking for my family and friends are the precious lingering memories. Eating in restaurants can be a wonderful experience but it doesn't match the enjoyment of entertaining at home.

When you are planning a menu, consider colour and texture, and choose one dish that dazzles. However competent you are, there is no need to prove it course after course. Time and time again, you will be encouraged in recipe books to prepare as much as you can ahead of time, and this is sound advice. Think through the dishes you plan to cook, prepare whatever you can in advance and lay the table the day before, if that is possible. Do not insist to yourself that all must be perfect, for this is a sure way to spoil the spirit of the occasion. Entertaining isn't about proving you are the world's best cook.

Cooking in advance allows you to focus on the important things – such as making guests feel welcome and at ease.

Cutlery and crockery need not be matching – in fact sometimes it is more charming when they are not.

As for the table setting, it is hard to beat generous-sized plates of a colour that does not contradict the food, simple glasses in which the glorious colour of the wine seems suspended, and large, generous soft napkins. Flowers cut from the garden – sitting lazily in a vase upon the table, rather than precisely arranged – lend character. Often when there is too much going on at the table, it feels as though too little has been done in the kitchen.

In my choice of recipes, I have included what seems important in terms of linking beautiful produce, food to share and memories. Afternoon tea is a treat that we rarely have these days, but it's lovely to savour dainty sandwiches and wonderful aromas of vanilla, spices and fragrant teas.

Candles lit in the evening lend a dream-like, almost smudgy, quality to everything around them, making things appear softer and warmer.

Special days, such as Christmas, Easter and birthdays, mark the passing of the year, so I have included menus for these. The Easter feast, Roman in feel, celebrates spring with lamb, tender artichokes and peas. An Italian rice cake, topped with candied citrus fruit, serves as dessert. Christmas Eve always feels romantic to me. Glistening food and glowing light enhance the anticipation: oysters served simply, richly glazed ham and spiced fruits, followed by an opulent pashka. Russian in origin, this dessert reminds me of deep snow, fur hats and horse-drawn carriages.

Good entertaining comes from imbuing an occasion with your own personal style. Cook and eat with gusto... and joy!

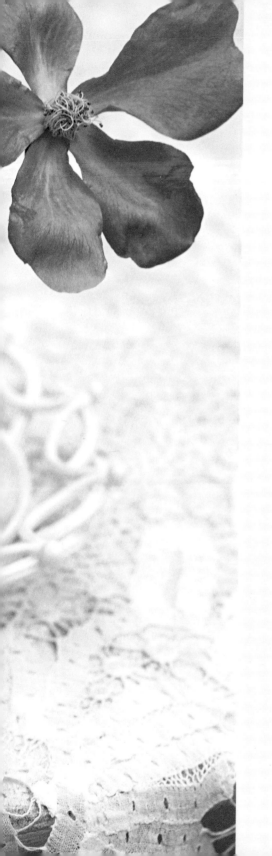

Breakfast

A long leisurely weekend breakfast, with time to eat in a relaxed manner, chatting to my family and reading the papers from cover to cover, is a real treat for me. Invariably during the week, I'm rushing around the house first thing in the morning, so breakfast is on the go – a hasty bowl of muesli or an inky black coffee and a piece of toast grabbed quickly and eaten in the car on the way to work. So to lay the table for breakfast, take a little time over preparing it and actually sit down and stop is both a pleasure and a necessity once in a while.

I love eggs – organic, free-range and as fresh as possible. At work we have our own chickens and, although they are very haphazard about producing eggs, it is sometimes possible to cook one or two still warm from laying – their yolks deep yellow in colour and their whites firm and bouncy.

Poached fruit is also a favourite, eaten with sheep's milk yoghurt and perhaps a sprinkling or two of toasted muesli, while my children adore pancakes for breakfast at the weekend.

Bircher muesli

I eat this creamy, good-for-you muesli, almost every weekday, all year round. On Sunday evening, I put a large tub of oats to soak that will last us through until Friday and keep it in the fridge. In the morning I add a spoonful or so of plain yoghurt, a drizzle of honey and whatever fruit is in season – strawberries, blueberries and raspberries in the summer; or stewed plums, apples or pears in autumn. Sweet tasting, packed full of goodness and sustaining enough to carry you through until lunchtime, it works a treat. The original recipe dates back to the 1890s and was created by Swiss Dr Bircher-Benner.

SERVES 4

250g whole rolled oats

grated zest of 1 lemon

grated zest and juice of 2 oranges

100ml water

2 sharp green dessert apples

500g plain yoghurt

100ml runny honey

2 tbsp chopped nuts, toasted

large handful of fruit, such as summer berries or 4 –6 tbsp poached autumn fruits

The night before, mix the oats, lemon and orange zest, orange juice and water together in a bowl. Cover and leave to soak overnight in the fridge.

In the morning, grate the apples, leaving the skin on. Add to the soaked oats, together with the yoghurt and honey, and mix well.

Divide the muesli among 4 bowls. Scatter over the chopped nuts and top with the fruit.

❁ Soaking oats overnight softens the texture, without adversely affecting their slightly nutty flavour. Folding in thick, creamy yoghurt, honey and seasonal fruit the following morning adds freshness and turns the cereal into a highly nutritious breakfast.

Strawberry, fig and greengage compote

This medley of late summer fruits can be varied according to the season. Later in the year, try pear and rhubarb, or quince and apple, or any combination of these fruits. The compote keeps well in the fridge for a day or two, so you can eat it whenever the fancy takes you.

SERVES 6–8

500g greengages, halved and stoned

100g caster sugar

3 tbsp water

8 figs

250g English strawberries

Greek-style yoghurt, to serve

Put the greengages into a saucepan with the sugar and water. Place over a medium-low heat and bring to the boil, then lower the heat and simmer for 10–12 minutes or until the greengages are just beginning to collapse. Remove from the heat and leave to cool for 5 minutes.

Tear the figs in half and stir them through the warm greengages; they will cook slightly in the warmth without falling apart. Halve the strawberries and add these too. Leave to cool completely, then cover and chill.

Remove the compote from the fridge about 10 minutes before serving. Accompany with a bowl of yoghurt.

Scrambled eggs with spinach and slow-roasted tomatoes

For me, scrambled eggs are only really good when they are creamy, glossy and luxurious. If eggs are cooked too much, I feel they lose their very nature. As with any dish that is essentially showcasing just one ingredient, that ingredient must be at its very best. A little patience is required when scrambling eggs in this fashion, but the end result is well worth the effort and the method is faultless.

SERVES 4

70g cold unsalted butter

8 very fresh organic free-range large eggs

sea salt and freshly ground black pepper

150g young leaf spinach, well washed

16–20 warm slow-roasted tomatoes (see page 245)

Grate 50g of the butter and set aside. Beat the eggs in a bowl, seasoning them well with salt and pepper.

Place a heavy-based, small-medium saucepan over a very low heat, add a third of the grated butter and allow it to just melt.

Pour in the beaten eggs and add a further teaspoonful of grated butter. Stir continuously, adding the butter in small increments; the eggs will gradually begin to scramble and thicken. Keep on adding the grated butter until it is all incorporated, at which point the eggs should be gloriously rich and soft enough to drop from a spoon; this will take about 10 minutes.

Meanwhile, cook the spinach, with just the water clinging to the leaves after washing, in a large saucepan over a medium heat for a few minutes until wilted. Drain in a sieve, pressing out as much water as possible.

Just before serving, melt the remaining butter in a pan, add the spinach and warm through gently. Season with salt and pepper to taste.

Spoon the creamy scrambled eggs onto warm plates and pile the spinach alongside. Grind over some pepper, add the warm slow-roasted tomatoes and serve at once.

There is a saying that if you have an egg in the house, you have a meal. True, of course, and you can eat eggs at any time of the day. In the morning they provide a concentrated source of protein and energy; in the evening they inspire a sense of warmth and comfort.

Banana bread

One of the most beautiful aromas in a kitchen is when an oven door is opened and the sweet smell of freshly cooked banana bread is released into the room. It has a warmth about it, a mixture of sponge, brown sugar and ripe bananas all rolled into one. It is almost impossible to eat just one slice. To fully appreciate their flavour, the bananas must be really ripe and soft; look for fruit with skins that are slightly bruised with a few black spots.

MAKES 8–9 SLICES

125g unsalted butter, softened, plus extra to grease

250g plain flour, plus extra to dust

4 ripe bananas, peeled

few drops of lemon juice

300g golden caster sugar

2 organic free-range large eggs

½ tsp vanilla extract

pinch of salt

1 tsp bicarbonate of soda

½ tsp ground cinnamon

125ml whole milk

75g light muscovado sugar

Preheat the oven to 190°C/Gas 5. Butter and flour a loaf tin, measuring approximately 20 x 10cm, and line the base with baking parchment. Mash the bananas with the lemon juice in a bowl, using a fork.

Beat the butter and caster sugar together in a large bowl, using an electric mixer if you wish, until pale and creamy. Beat in the eggs one by one, then incorporate the mashed bananas and vanilla extract.

Sift the flour, salt, bicarbonate of soda and cinnamon together over the mixture. Using a large metal spoon, fold in carefully, until evenly combined. Finally fold in the milk.

Spoon the mixture into the prepared loaf tin, gently spread level and scatter the muscovado sugar evenly over the surface. Bake on the middle shelf of the oven for 45 minutes, or until a skewer inserted into the centre comes out clean.

Leave the banana bread to cool in the tin for 10 minutes before turning out onto a wire rack to cool further. Best eaten slightly warm.

Apricot butter

Less sweet and intense in flavour than jam, butter laced with moistened dried fruit makes a nice change for breakfast. Flavoured butters appeal to me because they are not overwhelming in the way that a jam can be, and I like to appreciate the texture and flavour of good bread to the full. This smooth apricot butter is delectable spread on warm banana bread, crusty slices of sourdough or toasted rye bread; I also like to dollop it onto hot pancakes. Try using other dried fruits – plump soft prunes, sticky dates or dried figs, for example.

MAKES 350G

100g dried apricots

250g unsalted butter, softened

2–3 tsp icing sugar

Soak three-quarters of the dried apricots in enough warm water to cover for 20 minutes to soften. Chop the remaining apricots into small chunks and set aside.

Drain the soaked apricots and place in a food processor with the softened butter and 2 tsp icing sugar. Purée until smooth – the butter should be a pretty pale apricot colour. Taste for sweetness, blending in a little more icing sugar if required.

Transfer the butter to a bowl and stir in the chopped apricots. Use straight away or wrap in baking parchment (see below), seal and refrigerate.

This butter keeps well in the fridge for a week or so. Slice off as much as you need and leave at room temperature for about 10 minutes before using, to allow it to soften slightly.

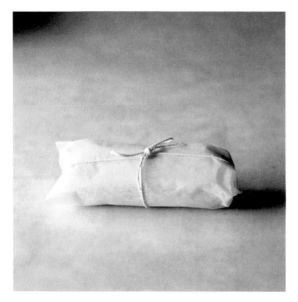

Flavoured butters are a simple and effective way of adding something a little special to anything they sit on top of. The butter adds a creamy delicate richness, while the flavours bound within are more of a hint – subtlety in cooking is often more rather than less. Once you've made the butter, spoon it onto a sheet of baking parchment on your work surface. Form the butter into a log shape using a spatula, then roll in the parchment, fold the ends to seal and place in the fridge.

Old-fashioned pancakes with maple syrup

For some reason I prefer to eat pancakes during the summer months, perhaps because I reminisce about eating them in the sunshine in Sydney around Christmas. That's when I have time to eat a long and languid breakfast, preferably after a swim in salty water, sitting in a towel watching the waves. Having said that, the best pancakes of all are made by my youngest daughter Evie – this is her recipe.

MAKES 12

250g plain flour

3 tsp baking powder

small pinch of salt

2½ tbsp caster sugar

2 organic free-range large eggs, lightly beaten

500ml whole milk

75g unsalted butter, melted, plus extra for brushing

To serve

75g unsalted butter, softened

1 tsp icing sugar, or to taste

maple syrup, to drizzle

Sift the flour, baking powder and salt into a large bowl and stir in the sugar. Make a well in the centre and add the eggs, milk and melted butter. Stir well to combine and make a smooth batter. Leave to rest for 20 minutes.

Meanwhile, sweeten the softened butter for serving with icing sugar to taste, beating well to combine and lighten.

Place a large non-stick frying pan over a medium-low heat. Brush the base with a little butter and when the pan is hot, ladle a small amount of batter into the centre of the pan.

Cook for about 2 minutes until bubbles begin to appear on the surface, indicating that the pancake is ready to turn. Using a spatula, gently turn the pancake and cook for a further 2 minutes.

Remove to a warm plate and keep warm in a low oven while you cook the other pancakes. Don't worry if the first pancake is disappointing; this is often the case – the rest will be perfect. As they are cooked, stack the pancakes interleaved with greaseproof paper on the plate in the oven.

Serve the warm pancakes topped with a knob of sweetened butter and a generous drizzle of maple syrup.

Sourdough toast with bananas, strawberries and ricotta

This quick and simple dish reminds me of Sydney, a city that does breakfast very well. If I happen to be there on a weekend morning, I'll often stop and breakfast at one of the sidewalk cafés, with the newspapers, watching the world go by. Like so many simple dishes, this one relies on using the best possible ingredients. It is a breakfast for the warmer summer months – when something cool, gently sweet and refreshing is called for. (Illustrated on previous page.)

SERVES 4

4 slices of crusted sourdough bread

2 bananas, peeled

12 strawberries

4 tbsp mild-flavoured honey

4 tbsp fresh ricotta (preferably buffalo milk)

a little lemon juice

Grill the sourdough bread on both sides until golden brown, then allow to cool slightly.

Split the bananas in half lengthways. Slice the strawberries in half.

Place a slice of sourdough toast on each plate and spread with some of the honey. Arrange the banana and strawberries on top, spoon on the ricotta and drizzle over the remaining honey. Finish with a little squeeze of lemon juice.

A medley of ricotta, honey and fruit is a lovely soft, sweet contrast to the crisp, slightly sour bread. Try other fruits – apricots, peaches, nectarines and raspberries – in any combination that appeals to you.

Cornbread

Originating from the southern states of America, cornbread is not often served at breakfast time, but it works for me – especially eaten fresh from the oven as a warming start to the day. It is particularly delicious with smoked chilli butter.

MAKES 10–12 SLICES

butter, to grease

250g plain flour, plus extra to dust

375g fine polenta or cornmeal

good pinch of sea salt

3 tsp baking powder

1 organic free-range large egg

300ml buttermilk, or whole milk with a few drops of lemon juice added

80ml corn oil

Preheat the oven to 200°C/Gas 6. Butter and flour a 23cm square baking tin, 4–5cm deep.

In a large bowl, combine the flour, polenta, salt and baking powder. Make a well in the centre.

Break the egg into a separate bowl and whisk lightly, then pour in the milk and oil and whisk to mix. Pour this liquid into the well in the dry ingredients and stir to combine.

Now pour the mixture into the prepared tin and place on the middle shelf of the oven. Cook for 25 minutes, or until golden brown on top and slightly shrunk from the sides of the tin. To test, insert a skewer into the middle; it should come out clean.

Leave the cornbread in the tin to cool for 10 minutes, then turn out onto a wire rack. Serve warm, cut into thick slices.

Chilli butter

The slightly sweet flavour and dense texture of cornbread calls for unctuous melting butter spiked with a little warmth. It's a lovely treat, especially on a cold winter's morning. You'll have more chilli butter than you need for your cornbread, but it keeps well in the fridge and is good with other things, such as savoury scones. I often use a generous knob to fry eggs – it lends a subtle hint of chilli.

MAKES 250G

1 fresh red chilli, deseeded

1 dried red chilli

250g unsalted butter, softened

1 tbsp sweet paprika

large pinch of rock salt

Preheat the grill to high and grill the fresh chilli, turning as necessary, until it is blistered and blackened all over. Set aside to cool.

Put the dried chilli in a small bowl, pour on a little boiling water and leave to soak for 10 minutes or so, until thoroughly softened. Drain and chop as finely as possible. Peel away the skin from the grilled chilli and chop it finely too.

Put the softened butter into a bowl. Add the chopped chillies, paprika and salt and stir well to combine. Lay a sheet of baking parchment on a work surface and spoon the flavoured butter onto the paper. Form into a log shape, using a spatula, then roll in the parchment, fold the ends to seal and keep in the fridge.

Remove the butter from the fridge 10 minutes before you are ready to use it to allow it to soften slightly.

Poached eggs and ham

I've always preferred poached eggs and ham to the more traditional eggs and bacon. Good-quality ham – sliced fairly thickly and gently browned in unsalted butter – has a sweeter flavour and a more interesting texture, which suits the delicate nature of poached eggs. The perfect poached egg can be elusive, but follow this method and you should be happy with the end result.

SERVES 4

200g piece of leg ham

4 organic free-range large eggs

1 tsp vinegar

25g unsalted butter

freshly ground black pepper

To serve

grilled or slow-roasted tomatoes (see page 245)

a little chopped parsley

Cut the ham, using a sharp knife, into slices about 3mm thick; allow 2–3 slices per person.

To poach the eggs, bring a fairly shallow, wide pan of water to a simmer with the vinegar added. One at a time, break the eggs into a cup and slip very gently into the simmering water. As soon as the last egg is in the pan, put the lid on and turn off the heat. Leave the eggs to cook in the residual heat: allow 3½ minutes for eggs that are still soft in the centre; 4 minutes for a slightly firmer egg.

Meanwhile, heat the butter in a non-stick frying pan until it begins to foam. Add the ham slices with a good grinding of black pepper and cook until lightly browned underneath, then turn and brown the other side.

When the eggs are ready, one at a time carefully remove with a slotted spoon, drain on kitchen paper and place on warm plates. Lay the ham alongside and serve, with grilled or slow-roasted tomatoes sprinkled with a little chopped parsley.

✽ Eggs for poaching must be very fresh – older eggs do not poach well and the whites have a tendency to disintegrate during cooking. Use a fairly shallow, lidded pan that is wide enough to take all 4 eggs and add a splash of vinegar to the water – this helps to seal the egg white. Don't add salt to the water as this breaks down the egg white.

Sunday lunch

Lunch on Sunday is the perfect way to round off a weekend – a good time to cook for friends and family. For me, entertaining at home is a yearning for intimacy and comfort – and to share those pleasures with others. Usually Sunday lunch has the added advantage of time – to lay the table just as you would have it and to cook in a way that is less hurried. And, of course, the pace of the meal itself can be slower and altogether more enjoyable.

In the summer when the weather is warm enough, I'll drag a table into the garden, fill a vase full of flowers and a jug full of home-made cordial. I find odd plates and glasses charming in this setting. Often I'll scatter a few cushion here and there to suggest that life has slowed down – for a little while, at least.

During the coldest months of winter, I like to serve lunch slightly later in the day, just as the afternoon light is beginning to fade. It's most definitely a time to relax in the warm and linger with your elbows on the table, reflecting that life is good after all.

Easy roast chicken

Roast chicken with anchovy butter
Grilled corn-on-the-cob
Ratatouille
New potatoes
*
Lemon self-saucing pudding

Roast chicken with anchovy butter

I grew up on roast chicken – always with mashed potatoes and green beans. My mother didn't do roast potatoes, and neither do I. This is how I like to serve roast chicken in the summer – the flavoured butter complements the sweetcorn accompaniment as well as the chicken. In the winter, I often roast pumpkin with red onions and sweet potatoes or fennel slices to serve instead. It's worth spending the extra on a good-quality chicken – free-range, organic and not too huge.

SERVES 6

1 organic free-range chicken, about 2kg

sea salt and freshly ground black pepper

extra virgin olive oil, to drizzle

Anchovy and herb butter

12 good-quality tinned anchovies or from a jar (Ortiz, for example)

2 garlic cloves, peeled and chopped

1 dried red chilli, crumbled, with seeds

1 tender rosemary stem, leaves only, finely chopped

finely grated zest of 1 lemon

200g unsalted butter, cut into small cubes

Season the chicken generously with salt inside and out – do this the night before if possible as it helps to tenderise the meat and season it right through. Wrap loosely and leave in the fridge overnight.

Take the chicken out the fridge 2 hours before putting it into the oven. Cut off the wing tips and neck, and tuck the neck flap of skin under the bird.

Preheat the oven to 180°C/Gas 4. Rub the chicken all over with olive oil. Place in a roasting tin large enough to hold it comfortably, laying the bird on one side. Roast on the middle shelf of the oven for 30 minutes, then turn the bird onto its other side and roast for a further 30 minutes. Finally turn the chicken on its back and roast for a final 20 minutes, or until cooked through. To test, pierce the thickest part of the thigh with a skewer – the juices should run clear. Turn off the oven and leave the chicken inside with the door slightly ajar to let it rest for at least 15 minutes.

Meanwhile, for the butter, put the anchovies, garlic, chilli, rosemary and lemon zest into a small saucepan over a low heat and stir gently until the anchovies begin to disintegrate. Now add the butter, a couple of cubes at a time, stirring as you do so, until it is all incorporated. This sauce should be made just before you are ready to eat, otherwise it is likely to split.

Transfer the chicken to a warm platter and spoon over some of the warm butter; pour the rest into a jug. Serve at once, with the accompaniments.

An anchovy butter makes a nice change with roast chicken, but I very often serve a simple gravy, prepared as follows: Pour off the fat from the roasting tin, then place it over a high heat on the hob. Pour in ⅓–½ bottle of dry white wine, scraping up the delicious bits that have gathered on the bottom of the tin with a wooden spoon as you do so. Let it bubble to reduce by half and serve alongside the chicken.

Grilled corn-on-the-cob

We grow corn in our garden, just enough to enjoy for a day or so, as it takes up space in a little garden. The plant has a pale green languid beauty. Try to buy ears of corn still in their husks – the heads should be tight and not too pale in colour. On a warm summer's day, you could cook these cobs on the barbecue, perhaps serving them as a starter in the garden before the roast. Be generous when seasoning – sea salt and chilli work so well with the sweetness of ripe corn.

SERVES 6

6 corn-on-the-cobs

75g unsalted butter, melted

1 red chilli, deseeded and finely sliced

sea salt

Add the corn-on-the-cobs to a pan of boiling water and parboil for about 15 minutes until almost tender.

Heat up your grill (or barbecue). Lay the corn cobs on the grill rack (or barbecue), but not too close to the heat source. Cook for 5 minutes or so, turning every minute, until charred on the outside.

Brush the corn with melted butter and sprinkle over the sliced chilli. Sprinkle with sea salt and serve while still nice and hot.

Ratatouille

I have always loved ratatouille. To me, it is a dish that suggests generosity and tastes of sunshine. And it is full of things I adore – aubergines, peppers and lots of basil. I prefer to cut the vegetables into fairly generous pieces and cook them gently, for longer than is usual – I find this allows their natural sweetness to shine, without compromising the individual flavours. It may sound like a contradiction, but somehow this dish manages to be punchy and mellow at the same time. It is good warm, but I think it is even better served at room temperature.

SERVES 6

1 tbsp extra virgin olive oil, plus a little extra to drizzle

2 red onions, peeled and finely sliced

small bunch of thyme

3 bay leaves

sea salt and freshly ground black pepper

1 aubergine

2 red peppers

1kg ripe small tomatoes

3 garlic cloves, peeled and crushed

5 courgettes

bunch of basil (ideally purple), leaves only

Warm the olive oil in a large heavy-based saucepan over a medium heat. Add the onions, thyme and bay leaves with a pinch of salt and sweat gently for 10 minutes, stirring every now and then to prevent the onions from sticking to the bottom of the pan.

While the onions are cooking, prepare the other vegetables. Halve the aubergine lengthways, then cut each piece into half-moon slices, 2cm thick. Halve the peppers lengthways and discard the core and seeds, then cut roughly into 2.5cm squares. Chop the tomatoes roughly into chunks.

Add the aubergine and red peppers to the onions in the pan along with the garlic and stir to combine. Now add the tomatoes to the pan and turn the heat down as low as possible. Put the lid on the pan and cook for 40 minutes, stirring from time to time.

Cut the courgettes into chunky rounds and add them the pan. Put the lid back on and cook very gently for a further 30 minutes. Discard the thyme sprigs and bay leaves.

Just before serving, taste and adjust the seasoning, adding a few grinds of pepper. Tear in the basil leaves and drizzle over a little extra olive oil.

Lemon self-saucing pudding

This homely, comforting pudding reminds me of growing up. It's the perfect end to a lazy Sunday lunch and you'll come across it on many a table in Australia. The top is the lightest sponge imaginable, yet dig deep with your spoon and you will find a creamy lemony sauce below. Sweet and tart all at once, it is delectable served warm with thick pouring cream.

SERVES 6

60g unsalted butter, at room temperature, plus extra to grease

200g caster sugar

finely grated zest and juice of 1 lemon

2 organic free-range large eggs, separated

4 tbsp self-raising flour, sifted

300ml whole milk

Preheat the oven to 180°C/Gas 4. Lightly butter a deep 1.5–1.8 litre ovenproof dish.

Using a hand-held electric whisk, cream the butter, sugar and lemon zest together in a bowl until well combined. Beat in the egg yolks, one by one.

Fold in the flour alternately with the milk to make a smooth batter. Gradually incorporate the lemon juice until evenly combined.

In a separate bowl, whisk the egg whites until they form firm peaks and then carefully fold into the mixture.

Pour into the prepared dish and stand in a roasting tin containing enough warm water to come halfway up the side of the dish. Bake on the middle shelf of the oven for about 50 minutes until risen and golden brown on top. Let stand for a few moments before serving.

✺ Whisked egg whites must be folded into a mixture very carefully in order to retain the air that has been incorporated into them during whisking. Using a large metal spoon or spatula, cut down through the mixture, then turn the spoon or spatula over as you lift it, scooping up the mixture and incorporating the egg whites as you do so. Continue until the mixture is evenly combined, light and fluffy. Keep the folding action gentle. The aim is to retain maximum volume and lightness.

Autumn flavours

Rabbit with endive and pancetta
Purée of parsnips
Pan-fried girolles
*
Date and sherry ice cream

Rabbit with endive and pancetta

This low-key Sunday lunch menu is stylish in its simplicity. I love the colours when all the dishes are laid together on the table. Caramel shades of brown and cream – quiet, subtle and heartwarming. I rarely cook with cream, but here a small amount of crème fraîche (lighter and slightly sour) is important. The flavours, like the colours, flow into each other – nothing asserts itself too strongly. Autumn is the season for wild mushrooms and the perfect time for this menu. If for some reason you don't want to cook rabbit, substitute a 1.5kg organic free-range chicken, cut into 8 pieces.

SERVES 4

2 small free-range farmed rabbits

20g unsalted butter

sea salt and freshly ground black pepper

6 slices of pancetta, derinded and sliced into 3mm strips

1 large shallot, peeled and finely chopped

3 garlic cloves, peeled and crushed

3 bay leaves

bunch of thyme

500ml good-quality chicken stock (preferably home-made)

3 heads of chicory (Belgium endive)

150ml crème fraîche

Place the rabbits on a board. Using a sharp knife, slice between the top of the thigh and the hip bone, snap the bone in between and continue to slice through until the leg separates easily from the body – do the same to the front legs. Set the saddles aside for another use (they are delicious grilled and tossed with salad leaves in a light dressing).

Place a large heavy-based pan over a low heat. Once the pan is warm, add the butter and let it melt. Season the rabbit all over with salt and pepper and brown in the butter, in batches if necessary, don't overcrowd the pan otherwise the meat will stew rather than brown well. Once the rabbit is a good colour all over, remove with a slotted spoon and set aside on a plate.

Now add the pancetta strips to the pan with the shallot, garlic, bay leaves and thyme. Cook gently for 10 minutes until the shallot is soft and translucent and the pancetta begins to impart a lovely smoky aroma.

Pour in the chicken stock and turn the heat up to medium. Return the rabbit to the pan, put the lid on and turn the heat right down. Cook very gently, stirring occasionally, for 1 hour.

Peel off and discard the outermost layer of the chicory bulbs, then slice each lengthways into about 6 strips. Add to the pan, stir and cook for a further 10 minutes.

Lastly spoon in the crème fraîche and stir well to combine. Season with plenty of black pepper and a little salt. Transfer to a warm serving dish.

I prefer to use farmed rather than wild rabbit. Gentler and less gamey in flavour, its flesh is sweeter. Rabbit needs to be either roasted (or grilled) quickly, or cooked slowly over a low heat for a substantial amount of time. It is the cooking in between that can make the meat tough.

Purée of parsnips

Parsnips have a wonderfully sweet nutty taste, which goes beautifully with rabbit, and conveniently this side dish can be prepared ahead of time. Unlike potatoes, parsnips may be puréed using a food processor – ensuring that the final texture is perfectly smooth. A good dollop of mustard stirred in just before serving adds a sharp depth that rounds off the flavour. Select parsnips that are blemish-free and small, yet feel heavy for their size.

SERVES 4

12 small parsnips

few thyme sprigs

sea salt and freshly ground black pepper

40g unsalted butter

120ml crème fraîche

1 heaped tbsp Dijon mustard

Peel the parsnips, halve lengthways and remove the central core, using a small knife, then cut into even-sized chunks. Place in a saucepan with the thyme and add sufficient cold water to cover. Add a generous pinch of salt and bring to the boil over a medium heat. Lower the heat and simmer for 25 minutes, or until the parsnip chunks fall apart when pierced with a fork. Drain thoroughly and discard the thyme.

Tip the parsnips into a food processor and add the butter, crème fraîche and a little salt and pepper. Purée until completely smooth, then add the mustard and process briefly until evenly combined.

Just before serving, reheat the parsnip purée very gently in a pan, stirring frequently so that it does not catch on the base of the pan.

Pan-fried girolles

Also known as golden chanterelles, girolles are my favourite mushrooms, along with porcini. Whereas porcini are deep and earthy, girolles are light, delicate and clean. Here they are cooked simply with mild olive oil, a little lemon juice, garlic and chopped parsley for a refined and elegant side dish. It is perfect with the rabbit, but also good just eaten on toast. This dish really needs to be cooked at the last minute for the flavour and texture of the girolles to be just right.

SERVES 4

1 tbsp mild-tasting extra virgin olive oil

500g girolles, cleaned (see opposite)

1 garlic clove, peeled and very finely chopped

few drops of lemon juice

sea salt and freshly ground black pepper

handful of flat-leaf parsley, leaves only, finely chopped

Warm a medium-large frying pan (preferably non-stick) over a medium heat, then add the olive oil. Once the oil is hot, add the mushrooms and cook for a couple of minutes; shake the pan once or twice but do not stir as this encourages them to emit water.

Now add the garlic, lemon juice, a generous pinch of salt and plenty of black pepper. Cook for a further minute or so, then stir in the chopped parsley. Taste and adjust the seasoning if necessary. Tip into a warm bowl and serve alongside the rabbit.

Mushrooms must be cleaned thoroughly before cooking, or else they are liable to have a gritty texture. Pick them over, removing any debris from the forest or woods using your fingers, then brush clean. You can buy a special soft mushroom brush if you like, though a pastry brush will do. The preparation may be a bit tedious but it's well worth the effort.

Date and sherry ice cream

This simple custard-based ice cream had a wonderfully rich, caramel flavour and a soft, silky texture. Pedro Ximénez is a luxurious, complex and sticky variety of sherry, tasting of dried fruit – raisins, prunes and dates, with which it is paired with here. It's never worth making ice cream in small quantities, so I've given a recipe that will provide enough for two meals for four. Eat within a couple of days of making.

SERVES 8

450ml double cream

150ml whole milk

1 vanilla pod, split lengthways

6 organic free-range large egg yolks

120g caster sugar

120g good-quality dates. such as Medjool

100ml Pedro Ximénez sherry

Pour the cream and milk into a heavy-based saucepan. Scrape the seeds from the vanilla pod and add them to the creamy milk with the empty pod. Place over a low heat and gently bring to just below the boil. Take off the heat and set aside to infuse for 15–20 minutes. Take out the vanilla pod.

Beat the egg yolks and sugar together in a bowl, using a whisk, until pale and thick. Gently reheat the creamy milk and pour slowly onto the whisked egg yolk mixture, stirring with the whisk as you do so.

Return the custard to the clean saucepan and place over the lowest possible heat. Using a wooden spoon, stir gently in a figure-of-eight motion until the custard thickens – this will take up to 10 minutes. The custard is ready when it is thick enough to coat the back of the wooden spoon. At this point immediately remove from the heat and strain the custard through a fine sieve into a cold bowl. Leave to cool completely.

Meanwhile, stone the dates and chop the flesh as finely as possible; place in a bowl. Warm the sherry very slightly in a pan and then pour over the chopped fruit. Set aside to macerate.

Once the custard is completely cool, pour into an ice-cream maker and churn according to the manufacturer's instructions. When the ice cream begins to set, add the date and sherry mixture and continue to churn for another 10 minutes.

Transfer the ice cream to a freezerproof container and place in the freezer until needed. Scoop into pretty glass dishes to serve.

When cooking a custard you need to use a gentle heat and be patient – don't be tempted to turn up the heat in order to cook it more quickly as you could easily end up with a scrambled mess. To test whether the custard is sufficiently cooked, check that it is thick enough to lightly coat the wooden spoon, then turn the spoon over and draw a line from one end to the other with your finger. If the custard doesn't run back in and fill the channel you've created, then the custard is ready.

Slow-roasted pork

Slow-cooked belly of pork
Gratin of white beans
Sautéed leeks

*

Fig tart

Slow-cooked belly of pork

A brittle, salty outer crust hiding layers of sweet, succulent meat beneath – this is the way I like to eat
pork belly. Overwhelmingly rich you might think, but small pieces are all that are needed accompanied
by a gratin of white beans and gently sautéed sweet, small leeks. If you prefer, serve simply roasted
potatoes and a lightly dressed green salad instead of the gratin – the vinegar in the dressing will help
to cut the richness of the meat.

SERVES 6

2kg pork belly, with skin
and ribs intact

2 tbsp olive oil

sea salt and freshly
ground black pepper

4 carrots, peeled and
roughly chopped

2 large red onions,
peeled and roughly
chopped

6 garlic cloves, skin on,
but lightly smashed

5 bay leaves

handful of rosemary
sprigs, leaves only,
roughly chopped

250ml verjus or dry
white wine

4 tbsp red wine vinegar

5 tbsp water

Preheat the oven to 200°C/Gas 6. Using a small sharp knife, score the skin
of the pork belly at 2cm intervals, making the cuts about 5mm deep. Rub
the olive oil and 1 tbsp sea salt into the skin.

Place the pork belly, skin side up, in a roasting tray large enough to hold
it comfortably. Roast on the middle shelf of the oven for 50 minutes until
the skin begins to colour and blister.

Carefully lift out the pork onto a board. Toss the vegetables, garlic and
herbs together in a bowl, then scatter over the base of the roasting tray.
Pour over the verjus or wine, wine vinegar and water. Lay the pork on top
of the vegetables and cover with foil.

Return the roasting tray to the middle shelf of the oven. Immediately turn
down the heat to 160°C/Gas 2½ and cook for a further 2¼ hours, turning
the vegetables from time to time.

Finally uncover the pork, turn the oven setting back up to 200°C/Gas 6
and cook for a further 15 minutes to brown the meat. Allow to rest in a
warm place for 20 minutes, then discard the vegetables and herbs.

Carve the pork into 2–3cm slices, sliding out the bones as you do so. Serve
with the accompaniments.

The advantage of cooking food that may be cooled and reheated just before serving is that the flavours will have found their feet together and often taste that much better for it.

Gratin of white beans

The pairing of roast meat with little dried or fresh beans works well and makes a pleasant change from potatoes – pale green flageolet beans with lamb is a lovely French example. You just need to remember to put the beans to soak the evening before. Conveniently, you can assemble this dish well in advance – ready to pop into the oven half an hour before you wish to eat.

SERVES 6

400g cannellini or other small dried white beans, soaked overnight in cold water

500ml double cream or crème fraîche

2 garlic cloves, peeled and crushed

bunch of thyme, leaves only

sea salt and freshly ground black pepper

100g fresh white breadcrumbs

100g Parmesan, freshly grated

40g unsalted butter, melted

Drain the beans, tip into a medium saucepan and pour on enough fresh water to come 2–3cm above the beans. Bring to the boil over a high heat, then immediately turn down the heat. Simmer until the beans are tender but not falling apart; this will take approximately an hour depending on how long the beans have been stored; begin checking after 50 minutes or so. If necessary, top up the water during cooking to keep the beans covered.

Preheat the oven to 200°C/Gas 6. Once the beans are tender, drain them in a colander and then tip into a bowl. Pour over the cream or crème fraîche and scatter over the crushed garlic and thyme leaves. Season generously with salt and pepper and mix together well. Transfer to a medium ovenproof dish.

For the topping, in a clean bowl, mix the breadcrumbs and grated Parmesan together lightly, using your fingers.

Scatter the topping over the beans and then trickle over the melted butter. Bake on the middle shelf of the oven for about 25 minutes until golden brown and bubbling.

Sautéed leeks

This is perhaps the nicest way to cook leeks and it goes with all manner of things – try it with roast chicken and a ripe tomato salad. The dish can be prepared ahead and reheated just before serving.

SERVES 6

12 small leeks

50g unsalted butter

bunch of thyme

60g Parmesan, freshly grated

sea salt and freshly ground black pepper

1 tbsp chopped parsley

First trim off the top of the leeks, leaving only a small amount of green, and trim the root end. Now slice the leek lengthways into quarters, cutting almost but not quite through to the base. Rinse well under cold running water, shaking to loosen any dirt.

Lay the leeks in a medium, shallow pan and pour in just enough water to cover. Bring to the boil over a high heat, then lower the heat to a simmer and cook, uncovered, until the water has reduced by a third. Add the butter and thyme and continue to cook until almost all the water has evaporated, leaving glossy, sweet, soft leeks. Discard the thyme.

Scatter over the Parmesan and season generously with pepper, adding a little salt only if needed. Sprinkle with the chopped parsley and serve.

Fig tart

This classic French tart – filled with pastry cream and topped with fresh fruit – is a lovely way to appreciate fruits that are in season. Vary the fruit accordingly – try halved ripe strawberries or whole raspberries, or lightly poached apricots, peaches or cherries. Serve the tart just as it is.

SERVES 6

Pastry

250g plain (unbleached) flour, sifted, plus extra to dust

125g unsalted butter, well chilled, cut into small cubes

1 tbsp caster sugar

1 tsp vanilla extract

1 organic free-range large egg yolk

a little iced water

Pastry cream

320ml whole milk

3 organic free-range large egg yolks

2–3 drops of vanilla extract

3 tbsp caster sugar

3 tbsp plain flour

15g chilled unsalted butter, in pieces

Topping

8 perfectly ripe figs

1 tbsp fig, strawberry or raspberry jam

2 tbsp water

To make the pastry, tip the flour into a food processor and add the chilled butter, sugar and vanilla extract. Pulse until you have the consistency of course breadcrumbs. Add the egg yolk and 1 tbsp iced water and pulse once more; the pastry should begin to come together. Add a little more iced water as necessary, pulsing until the pastry forms a ball. (Be careful not to add too much water, as wet dough is difficult to work with.)

Wrap the pastry in baking parchment or cling film and leave to rest in the fridge for 30 minutes.

To make the pastry cream, gently warm the milk in a saucepan over a low heat until it just emits a little steam. Meanwhile, whisk the egg yolks, vanilla extract, sugar and flour together in a bowl to combine. Slowly pour on the warm milk, whisking as you do so.

Pour the mixture back into the pan and stir continuously over a low heat, using a wooden spoon in a figure-of-eight motion, until the custard thickens enough to coat the back of the spoon and no longer tastes floury; this will take about 10 minutes. Immediately pour through a sieve into a clean bowl and whisk in the chilled butter. Leave to cool completely, then cover the surface with baking parchment or cling film and refrigerate.

Roll out the pastry on a floured surface to a large round, about 3mm thick. Carefully lift the dough onto the rolling pin and drape it over a 25cm fluted flan tin, about 3cm deep. Press the pastry gently into the fluted sides and prick the base with a fork. Return to the fridge to chill for a further 30 minutes.

Preheat the oven to 180°C/Gas 4. Line the pastry case with greaseproof paper and baking beans (or raw chickpeas, beans or rice) and bake 'blind' on the middle shelf of the oven for 20 minutes. Remove the paper and beans and return to the oven for a further 15 minutes, or until the pastry is cooked through, golden brown and crisp. Transfer to a wire rack and leave to cool completely.

Spoon the pastry cream into the cooled pastry case and spread it evenly. Slice the figs across into rounds and lay them, overlapping, on top of the pastry cream in a circular pattern. Warm the jam with the water in a small pan, stirring to dissolve, then bring to the boil. Remove from the heat and allow the glaze to cool slightly.

Using a pastry brush, gently brush the figs with the glaze – this will give them a luxurious gloss. Cut into generous slices to serve.

Handle pastry as little as possible and with care. Don't worry if it breaks a little as you are in the process of lining the flan tin – simply patch it up as necessary.

It is important to rest pastry in the fridge once it is made and again after shaping, to minimise shrinkage during cooking – don't skip these stages.

Pastry should be cooked until it is golden brown and has a biscuity texture. There is really nothing more unpalatable than undercooked pastry.

Greek-style roast lamb

Crying lamb
Warm squash, mâche and hazelnut salad
*
Crème caramel with Pedro Ximénez

Crying lamb

I first tasted this wonderful dish when a friend in Sydney cooked it for me, a long time ago; she had acquired the recipe from a Greek friend. The lamb is cooked on a rack that sits above the dish of potatoes and tomatoes, thereby dripping its lovely juices upon them and imparting the most delicious flavours. It needs only a simple salad alongside, although almost any green vegetable could be served as a warm accompaniment if you prefer.

SERVES 6

1 leg of lamb, about 2kg

sea salt and freshly ground black pepper

1.5kg firm-textured, fairly waxy potatoes, such as Desirée or Roseval

700g ripe tomatoes, such as San Marzano

small bunch of marjoram or oregano, leaves only

3 garlic cloves, peeled and finely chopped

1 dried chilli, crumbled

40ml olive oil

small handful of good-quality black olives (optional)

Preheat the oven to 220°C/Gas 7. Trim the lamb of most of its surface fat, leaving a thin covering – to baste the joint during cooking. Season well all over with salt and pepper.

Wash the potatoes and pat dry, but don't bother to peel them. Slice into 3mm thick rounds and place in a large bowl. Slice the tomatoes into fairly thick rounds and add them to the potatoes. Scatter over the marjoram or oregano, garlic and dried chilli. Season with salt and pour over the olive oil. Toss together well, using your hands.

Tip the seasoned potatoes and tomatoes into a large roasting tray and spread them out evenly. Scatter over the olives if using. Set a robust wire rack (large enough to take the lamb) on top.

Place the lamb on the rack, cover with foil and carefully place on the middle shelf of your oven. Roast for 30 minutes.

Turn the oven setting down to 190°C/Gas 5. Remove the foil and roast for a further 1 hour, by which time the lamb should be cooked through and soft but still just slightly pink, while the potatoes will be soft and golden in colour. Remove from the oven and leave to stand for 15 minutes.

Lift the lamb onto a warm serving platter and surround with the potatoes and tomatoes. Carve the meat at the table.

When you are planning a Sunday lunch – or any other menu – it goes without saying that you need to choose dishes that work well together in terms of texture and flavour. But you should also consider how easily they can be prepared and cooked with the equipment you have to hand. Avoid having lots of dishes that need to be in the oven at the same time or a hob full of pans, which could prove difficult to manage. Think through the practicalities of your planned menu before you shop and cook.

Warm squash, mâche and hazelnut salad

Onion squash, which has a deep and not-too-sweet flavour, is my favourite squash variety ; its thin skin is best left on during roasting. Mâche, also known as lamb's lettuce, is slightly crunchy and has a very clean flavour. Tossed together in a hazelnut vinaigrette with crunchy toasted hazelnuts, these ingredients marry beautifully, creating a delicious and unusual accompaniment for the lamb.

SERVES 6

1 onion squash

40ml olive oil

1 dried chilli

sea salt

2 handfuls of mâche
(lamb's lettuce)

30g hazelnuts, toasted
and roughly chopped

Hazelnut vinaigrette

½ tbsp Dijon mustard

1½ tbsp good-quality red
wine vinegar

sea salt and freshly
ground black pepper

5 tbsp hazelnut oil

Preheat the oven to 200°C/Gas 6. Cut the squash in half and scoop out the seeds, then slice each half into 4–6 wedges, leaving on the thin skin. Place in a bowl and drizzle over the olive oil, crumble over the chilli and season with salt. Toss together well and then place in a roasting tin.

Cover the tin with foil and place in the oven. Roast for 20 minutes, then remove the foil and roast for a further 25 minutes, or until the squash is tender but not falling apart.

Meanwhile, for the hazelnut dressing, whisk the mustard and wine vinegar together in a bowl with a little salt and plenty of black pepper. Slowly pour in the hazelnut oil, whisking as you do so. Set aside.

Carefully wash the mâche, gently pat dry with a tea towel and place in a bowl. Pour on the dressing and toss gently.

Toss some of the salad leaves into a shallow serving dish and arrange the roasted squash on top. Scatter over the rest of the leaves and finish with a sprinkling of chopped toasted hazelnuts.

Toasting nuts or just warming them in the oven releases their flavour. Spread the nuts out on a baking tray and toast in the oven preheated to 180°C/Gas 4 for 3–4 minutes, or longer for a deeper colour.

Crème caramel with Pedro Ximénez

I love the silky texture of a baked rich creamy custard and the way it wobbles prettily on a plate. The bittersweet caramel that sits atop adds a real intensity too. The deep mellow flavour of Pedro Ximénez sherry – trickled over just before serving – is a lovely enhancement but you can serve the crème caramel just as it is if you prefer.

SERVES 6

500g caster sugar

500ml whole milk

500ml double cream

2 organic free-range large eggs

9 organic free-range large egg yolks

about 2 tbsp Pedro Ximénez sherry

Preheat the oven to 170°C/Gas 3. Have ready 6 dariole moulds or ramekins (200ml capacity).

To make the caramel, put 300g of the sugar into a medium heavy-based saucepan and melt over a medium heat. Cook to a dark golden caramel, swirling the pan occasionally as the sugar begins to colour. Watch carefully and remove from the heat as soon as the caramel is dark golden; this will take about 5 minutes. Don't let it darken too much otherwise it will taste bitter. Quickly, but carefully (as the caramel will be hot), spoon 2 tbsp into the base of each mould. Stand the moulds in a roasting tin and set aside.

For the custard, pour the milk and cream into a saucepan and bring just to a simmer over a medium heat, then take off the heat. Meanwhile, lightly whisk the whole eggs, egg yolks and remaining sugar together in a bowl, just to combine. Slowly pour in the warm milk, whisking as you do so.

Pour the custard into a clean heavy-based saucepan and stir over a very low heat with a wooden spoon for 10 minutes or so until it is thick enough to lightly coat the back of the spoon. Ladle the custard onto the caramel base in the prepared moulds, filling them almost to the rim.

Pour enough hot water into the roasting tin to come halfway up the side of the moulds. Bake on the middle shelf of the oven for 1 hour. To test, insert a small sharp knife into the centre of one of the puddings; if it comes out clean, the custard is set. Leave the dishes in the bain-marie to cool slowly to room temperature, then take them out and chill in the fridge overnight.

To serve, run a knife around the inside of each mould and invert onto a plate – the set custards should slip out easily. Spoon a teaspoonful or so of sherry over the top of each one and serve.

✿ Cooking in a bain-marie is a way of protecting a delicate dish (or individual dishes) from the direct, intense heat of the oven; it is also used to keep sauces warm once they are cooked. A bain-marie (literally a water-bath) surrounds the dishes with gentle steam.

Mediterranean fish lunch

Bouillabaisse
Rouille
Chicory salad
*
Rich chocolate pots

Bouillabaisse

There are many versions of this famous dish from the South of France, some with potatoes and/or wine; I prefer mine without either – the simplicity appeals to me. Along the Mediterranean, species such as rascasse, mullet, red gurnard and wrasse are used, but you can vary the fish according to availability.

Traditionally, bouillabaisse is eaten in two parts. First most of the broth is served as a soup, with rouille and toast on the side. This is followed by the fish and shellfish (illustrated overleaf), which have been kept moist in some of the broth. Two courses with only one pan to wash – my dream Sunday lunch.

SERVES 6

2kg mixed fish and shellfish, such as sea bass, red mullet, turbot, live langoustines and fresh clams, cleaned

125ml olive oil

2 large yellow onions, peeled and finely sliced

35 saffron strands

4 garlic cloves, peeled and smashed

500g ripe tomatoes, roughly chopped

1.25 litres water

4 bay leaves

peel of 1 orange

handful of fennel fronds, ideally wild (optional)

sea salt and freshly ground black pepper

To serve

Rouille (see page 70)

1 pagnotta or baguette, sliced and toasted

olive oil, for brushing

Cut the fish into tranches, about 5cm wide, retaining the bones as these lend flavour. Split the langoustines in half lengthways.

Heat 1 tbsp of the olive oil in a large saucepan over a low heat. Add the onions and sweat gently for 5 minutes until tender but not brown. Stir in the saffron and garlic, then increase the heat to medium and cook for a further 5 minutes, stirring occasionally.

Add the tomatoes, water, bay leaves and orange peel to the pan and bring to the boil. Cook at a moderate boil for 5 minutes, then add the pieces of fish, lower the heat and simmer for 5 minutes.

Finally, add the langoustines, clams, fennel if using, and the rest of the olive oil. Cover and cook steadily for 4–5 minutes until the clams open and the langoustines turn pink. Season with salt and pepper to taste.

Serve the broth in warm bowls with rouille and toasted baguette slices brushed with olive oil, followed by the fish and shellfish as a main course.

Toasted baguette is the classic bread to use here, but I prefer
the texture and crunch of toasted pagnotta. Feel free to choose.

Rouille

Serve this alongside the fish broth and pass it around so that everyone can take a dollop and stir it in.

SERVES 6

1 red pepper

1 red chilli

2 garlic cloves, peeled and crushed

2 organic free-range large egg yolks

1 tbsp good-quality red wine vinegar

2 tbsp fresh breadcrumbs

sea salt and freshly ground black pepper

120ml extra virgin olive oil

Preheat the grill to high. Grill the red pepper and chilli until blackened all over, turning as necessary. Place in a bowl, cover with cling film and leave to cool slightly; the steam will help to loosen the skins. Peel away the skin from both and discard the seeds.

Put the red pepper, chilli, garlic, egg yolks, wine vinegar and breadcrumbs into a blender and add a little salt and pepper. Then turn on the machine and slowly drizzle in the olive oil through the funnel, as for making mayonnaise (this is an emulsified sauce).

Once all of the oil is added, turn off the machine and adjust the seasoning to taste. Spoon the rouille into a serving bowl.

Chicory salad

As bouillabaisse is so much a dish unto itself, a simple salad – with a distinctly French feel – is all that is needed. Chicory, with its slightly bitter taste and welcome crunch, is perfect here. Serve it after the bouillabaisse as opposed to alongside – for it deserves a place all on its own.

SERVES 6

2 heads of chicory

Vinaigrette

1 tbsp Dijon mustard

2 tbsp white wine vinegar

2 tsp crème fraîche

sea salt and freshly ground black pepper

80ml mild-tasting extra virgin olive oil

Rinse the chicory, then drain and gently pat dry. Slice into 1cm lengths and pile onto a serving plate.

For the vinaigrette, in a bowl, whisk the mustard, wine vinegar and crème fraîche together with a little salt and pepper to combine. Slowly drizzle in the olive oil, whisking as you do so. You should end up with a thick, creamy dressing.

Spoon the vinaigrette over the chicory and serve.

Rich chocolate pots

These little chocolate pots are rich and decadent, but each ramekin holds no more than a few mouthfuls. A lovely indulgent way to round off a meal.

SERVES 6

125g good-quality bitter chocolate, such as Valrhona, coarsely chopped

300ml double cream

300ml whole milk

50g caster sugar

6 organic free-range large egg yolks

1½ tbsp Cointreau or Grand Marnier

Preheat the oven to 150°C/Gas 2. Melt the chocolate together with half of the cream in a heatproof bowl set over a pan of gently simmering water, making sure that the bowl is not in direct contact with the water. Stir occasionally and, once the chocolate has melted, remove from the heat.

Warm the remaining cream with the milk and sugar in a small saucepan, stirring, until the sugar has dissolved. Whisk the egg yolks in a bowl and then pour on the warm milk mixture, whisking as you do so. Pour the mixture through a fine sieve onto the melted chocolate, stirring all the time to combine. Finally stir in the liqueur.

Spoon the mixture into 6 ramekins or custard pots and stand them, a little apart, in a roasting tin. Pour enough hot water into the roasting tin to come halfway up the side of the ramekins. Bake on the middle shelf of the oven for about 45 minutes until the custard is just set around the edges but still soft in the centre.

Leave the custards to cool in the bain-marie; they will continue to firm up as they cool. They will keep well for several days in the fridge, though they are nicest eaten a few hours after removing from the oven.

Alfresco eating

Eating outside – under clear blue skies, leafy trees and dappled sunlight – must be one of the great joys of summer. The day, however, must not be too scorching hot, and some shade is imperative, as eating in direct heat can be uncomfortable and tiring. The food is best served at room temperature, unless you are eating in the evening, when hot food may be just what is called for. The warmth of the day gives the opportunity for food to be enjoyed at its very best. In my view, food that is neither too hot nor too cold tastes more of itself.

A particularly glorious outdoor meal is a whole fish roasted with plenty of fresh herbs and generous slices of lemon, served with roasted fennel. Mayonnaise – made with mild extra virgin olive oil, the freshest organic eggs and a little squeeze of lemon juice – is the perfect accompaniment.

Remember to chill rosé and white wine in advance and have plenty of iced water to hand. For those who prefer not to drink alcohol during the day, serve a refreshing raspberry or elderflower cordial or home-made lemonade.

Mediterranean flavours

Roasted sea bass with lemon and thyme

Roasted fennel

Green beans with roasted tomatoes and olives

Mayonnaise

*

Mint ice cream

Roasted sea bass with lemon and thyme

A lovely summery dish to serve when fresh herbs are at their best. To make it easier on yourself, ask the fishmonger to scale and gut the fish for you.

SERVES 6

1 sea bass, about 2kg, cleaned

2 lemons

bunch of flat-leaf parsley

small bunch of lemon thyme

bunch of basil

2 tbsp extra virgin olive oil

sea salt and freshly ground black pepper

1 dried red chilli

Preheat the oven to 200°C/Gas 6. Rinse the fish inside and out under cold running water, then gently pat dry using a clean cloth. Lay the fish in a roasting tin, large enough to hold it comfortably. Slice the lemons thinly into rounds, 3mm thick.

Stuff the fish cavity with the herbs and about two-thirds of the lemon slices. Rub the skin of the fish with the olive oil, then season generously with salt and a little pepper. Lay the rest of the lemon slices on top and crumble over the dried chilli.

Roast on the middle shelf of the oven for 25 minutes, or until the skin is golden and the fish is cooked through. To test, pierce with a little knife to touch the backbone; the knife point should feel warm when removed and the flesh should be slightly steaming. Set aside to cool.

When ready to serve, very carefully transfer the fish to a platter and surround with the roasted fennel. Serve with mayonnaise and green beans with roasted tomatoes and olives.

Roasted fennel

Fennel and fish is a marriage made in heaven. You'll find it more convenient to roast the fennel separately from the fish, as it needs to be covered to begin with.

SERVES 6

6 fennel bulbs

2 tbsp olive oil

1 dried red chilli

sea salt and freshly ground black pepper

Preheat the oven to 200°C/Gas 6. Slice off the base of the fennel and remove the tough outer layer. Halve the bulbs lengthways and then cut into wedges. Place in a bowl and pour over the olive oil. Crumble over the chilli, season with salt and toss together, then transfer to a roasting tin.

Cover with foil and bake for 20 minutes, then remove the foil and return to the oven for a further 20 minutes. Allow to cool to room temperature.

Arrange the fennel around the roasted whole fish to serve.

✺ Don't feel disheartened if for some reason the mayonnaise begins to curdle, as this has happened to me many times. You can usually rectify it by spooning out the mayonnaise into a bowl, washing and drying the blender, then adding a fresh egg yolk to the machine and pouring in the curdled mayonnaise as slowly as possible through the funnel, with the motor running. Finally incorporate any remaining oil.

Green beans with roasted tomatoes and olives

French beans are equally good served hot or at room temperature and either way they can be cooked in advance. You do, however, need to keep a close eye on them: undercook and they will be too crunchy, cold in the middle and slightly raw-tasting; overcook and they are likely to be waterlogged and taste rather dull. The idea is to boil them to exactly the right point and then immediately refresh them under cold water – both to stop the cooking process and to retain their vivid green colour.

If serving the beans at room temperature, as here, dress them just beforehand. If serving hot, gently warm them in a pan with a little olive oil, a pinch of salt and plenty of pepper, sprinkling over a finely chopped garlic clove if you like.

SERVES 6

handful of baby plum tomatoes

splash of olive oil

sea salt and freshly ground black pepper

1kg fine French beans

50ml extra virgin olive oil

2 tsp red wine vinegar

20 or so little olives preserved in olive oil (ideally from Liguria or Provence)

40g Parmesan cheese, freshly grated (optional)

Preheat the oven to 170°C/Gas 3. Wash the tomatoes, pat dry and pierce once or twice, using a small sharp knife. Place on a baking tray, drizzle with a little olive oil and season with salt and pepper. Roast for 15 minutes or until soft, then set aside to cool.

Place a large pot of well-salted water on to boil. Top the beans, but don't tail them – it isn't necessary and they look pretty with the tails left on. When the water comes to a rolling boil, plunge in the beans and cook for 4 minutes, or until they are just tender to the bite and bright green in colour. Drain into a colander and immediately refresh under cold running water or in a bowl of iced water. Once the beans are cool, drain thoroughly and pat dry with a clean cloth.

Just before serving, pour over the extra virgin olive oil and wine vinegar and stir through the tomatoes, olives and Parmesan if using. Taste and adjust the seasoning – you will need pepper for sure, but the olives and Parmesan may provide enough salt.

Mayonnaise

The quickest, most foolproof way to make a mayonnaise is in a blender. The secret is to add the oil as slowly as possible through the funnel – pouring the oil from a jug makes it easier to control the flow.

SERVES 6

3 organic, free-range medium egg yolks

juice of 1 lemon

sea salt and freshly ground black pepper

250ml mild-tasting extra virgin olive oil, such as Ligurian

Put the egg yolks into a blender or small food processor and add the lemon juice and a good pinch each of salt and pepper. Whiz briefly, just to combine.

With the motor running, very slowly pour in the olive oil through the funnel – a few drops at a time to begin with, then in a thin stream – until it is all incorporated and you have a thick, glossy mayonnaise.

Mint ice cream

The beauty of this ice cream lies in its simple, clean taste – the flavour of the mint subtly shining through and lending character. You can make the custard a day in advance and keep it covered in the fridge until ready to use.

SERVES 6

Custard base

600ml whole milk

1 vanilla pod, split lengthways

6 organic free-range large egg yolks

100g caster sugar

Mint flavouring

220g caster sugar

500ml water

bunch of mint

For the custard base, pour the milk into a heavy-based saucepan and place over a low heat. Scrape the seeds from the vanilla pod and add them to the milk. Slowly bring to a simmer, then immediately remove from the heat and set aside to infuse for 20 minutes.

Meanwhile, whisk the egg yolks and sugar together in a bowl until thick and pale. Gently reheat the infused milk, then slowly pour onto the egg yolk mixture, stirring with the whisk as you do so. Return the custard to the pan and place over a very low heat. Stir with a wooden spoon, using a figure-of-eight motion, until the custard is thick enough to coat the back of the spoon, about 6–8 minutes; don't allow to overheat or it will curdle.

As soon as the custard has thickened, remove from the heat, strain through a fine sieve into a bowl and set aside to cool.

For the mint flavouring, put the sugar and water into a saucepan and dissolve over a medium heat. Add half the bunch of mint and bring to the boil. Lower the heat and simmer for 15 minutes, then set aside to cool. Once cooled, remove the mint and add a quarter of the syrup to the custard base. (Keep the rest in the fridge and use as a cordial, or add to iced tea for a refreshing drink.)

Pour the minted custard into an ice-cream maker and churn, according to the manufacturer's instructions, until the ice cream is thick enough just to drop from a spoon. Meanwhile, strip the leaves from the rest of the mint bunch and chop them finely.

Add the chopped mint to the ice cream and churn for a few more minutes to distribute the mint evenly. Cover and place in the freezer until the ice cream is thick enough to scoop. Serve piled into ice-cold glasses.

A moveable feast

A trug of little vegetables with aïoli

*

Poached langoustines
with green goddess dressing

Salad of Jersey Royals
with herbs and crème fraîche

Swiss chard with Parmesan

*

Roasted caramelised peaches

Shortbread

A trug of little vegetables with aïoli

Sweet young vegetables – prettily arranged in baskets and accompanied by nothing more than a rich, verdant aïoli – make perfect outdoor food. A grassy extra virgin olive oil is essential for the aïoli, as it lends an unctuous depth of flavour – a bland mayonnaise misses the point completely. You can make the aïoli a couple of hours in advance.

SERVES 6

a selection of vegetables, such as small carrots, quartered baby fennel bulbs, crisp chicory and treviso leaves, little ripe plum tomatoes on the vine, cucumber, chicory, broad beans and peas

Aïoli

3 small organic free-range egg yolks

2 garlic cloves, peeled and crushed

juice of ½ lemon

sea salt and freshly ground black pepper

200ml extra virgin olive oil

To make the aïoli, put the egg yolks into a blender or small food processor and add the crushed garlic and lemon juice. Season with a good pinch of salt and one or two generous grindings of pepper. Pour the olive oil into a jug. With the motor running, very slowly pour the olive oil through the funnel onto the egg yolks – drip by drip to begin with, then in a slow trickle – until it is all incorporated and you have a thick, glossy aïoli.

Spoon the aïoli into a bowl, or a plastic container if you are packing a picnic, and refrigerate until ready to serve or go.

Carefully wash all the vegetables and pat dry. Now simply take your prettiest basket, line it with a cloth and arrange the vegetables as you see fit.

You can either carry this meal out into the garden or pack it up to take on a picnic. You'll need a coolbox to transport most of the items, particularly the seafood, but the vegetables can be taken in their basket and the shortbread can go in a small tin in the picnic basket.

Poached langoustines with green goddess dressing

I like to eat shellfish on a picnic. The shells are perfect vehicles of transportation, their flesh is sweet and delicate, and they can be eaten in just two bites. If langoustines are not available, you can use prawns instead here, reducing the cooking time by a minute or two. Green goddess dressing is an American invention that intrigued me for a long time because of its exotic name. I came across it for the first time not long ago and after a few adjustments have made it ever since.

SERVES 6

24 langoustines
(allow 4 per person)

sea salt

a little chopped parsley
(optional)

Green goddess dressing

200ml home-made
mayonnaise (see
page 81)

1 tsp capers, well rinsed
and finely chopped

4 good-quality tinned
anchovies or from a jar
(Ortiz, for example),
finely chopped

small bunch of chives,
finely chopped

1 garlic clove, peeled and
finely chopped

few drops of Tabasco

50ml crème fraîche

squeeze of lemon juice

To make the dressing, put the mayonnaise into a bowl and stir in the capers, anchovies, chives, garlic and Tabasco until evenly combined. Stir in the crème fraîche and lemon juice, then taste and add a little salt if necessary.

Place a large pan of well salted water on to boil – it should be almost as salty as the sea. Once it is boiling vigorously, plunge in the langoustines and poach for 4 minutes. Scoop the shellfish out of the water and leave them to cool to room temperature.

Once cool, seal in a plastic container and keep in the fridge until you are ready to eat, or pack your picnic. Scatter over a little chopped parsley before serving if you wish.

It goes without saying

that langoustines must be absolutely fresh and you should check with your fishmonger that they were alive when they came into the shop. Ideally, cook them as soon as possible after buying, but if you need to store them until later in the day, lay them in the fridge, covered with damp newspaper.

Salad of Jersey Royals with herbs and crème fraîche

There's no mistaking the taste of Jersey Royals, which is derived from the rich fertile soil on Jersey where, naturally enough, they are grown. The potatoes are the colour of the island's earth and have a papery skin so thin that you can remove it with your fingers.

SERVES 6

1kg Jersey Royals (or other early new potato)

sea salt and freshly ground black pepper

2 tbsp extra virgin olive oil

juice of ½ lemon

Dressing

250ml crème fraîche

finely grated zest of 1 lemon

bunch of chives, very finely chopped

bunch of chervil, leaves only, finely chopped

small bunch of flat-leaf parsley, leaves only, finely chopped

Wash the potatoes thoroughly under cold running water, rubbing them well with your fingers to remove all traces of soil.

Bring a large saucepan of water to the boil and season liberally with salt. When the water comes to the boil, drop in the potatoes and cook until just tender when pierced with a knife; this will take about 15 minutes.

Drain and dress while still hot with the olive oil and lemon juice, then season with a little more salt and plenty of pepper. Set aside to cool.

Meanwhile, for the dressing, put the crème fraîche into a bowl with the lemon zest and chopped herbs. Mix well, seasoning with salt and pepper to taste. If it's a picnic you're planning, pack the dressing in a plastic tub. Refrigerate until needed.

Spoon the creamy herb dressing onto the potatoes to serve.

Early new potatoes, including Jersey Royals, are added to boiling water. This is the one exception to the rule that potatoes go into cold water.

Swiss chard with Parmesan

Chard is lovely – both warm and at room temperature. Dressed with olive oil and a squeeze of lemon juice it can be eaten just as it is or tossed through other vegetables. Here I have served it on its own, as an accompaniment to langoustines.

SERVES 6

2 large bunches of Swiss chard

sea salt and freshly ground black pepper

3 tbsp fruity extra virgin olive oil

juice of ½ lemon

30g Parmesan, freshly grated

There are two types of chard. Rainbow chard has beautiful brightly coloured stalks of pink, orange and yellow, while Swiss chard has a thick, cream central stalk that must be cooked separately from its leaves. Of the two, I generally prefer the Swiss variety.

Put a large saucepan of well-salted water on to boil. Wash the chard well under cold running water and shake off the excess. Lay the chard on a board and slice down either side of the central stalk, using a small sharp knife, to separate the leaves from the stalk. Set the leaves aside. Slice the stalks into short lengths on the diagonal.

Once the water is boiling, plunge in the stalks and cook for 3 minutes. Scoop out the chard stalks, using tongs or a slotted spoon, and place in a bowl. Immediately dress with half the olive oil, lemon juice and Parmesan. Season with salt and pepper and toss to combine, then set aside while you cook the leaves.

Add the chard leaves to the boiling water (in which the stalks were cooked) and blanch for 1½ minutes until wilted. Drain well, add to the cooked stalks and dress with the remaining olive oil, lemon juice and Parmesan. Set aside to cool.

Roasted caramelised peaches

Food to be eaten outdoors should not involve too much effort. After all, a picnic by its very nature is a relaxed and lazy affair. There is little work involved here but the final result is lovely. The peaches have a scent of summer about them and slip down your throat irresistibly. This is one of those desserts that works well served chilled – the peaches are sweeter, firmer and cleaner tasting savoured this way.

SERVES 6

6 peaches

6 tbsp Pedro Ximénez sherry

6 tsp soft brown sugar

pared zest of 1 lemon

1 vanilla pod, split in half lengthways

Preheat the oven to 200°C/Gas 6. Using a small sharp knife, cut the peaches in half and carefully prise out the stone. Lay the peach halves, rounded side down, in a roasting tray in which they fit quite snugly. Drizzle the sherry evenly over them and sprinkle with the brown sugar. Tuck in the strip of lemon zest and vanilla pod.

Cover with foil, sealing it tightly under the rim of the roasting tray and place on the middle shelf of the oven. Roast for 10 minutes, then remove the foil and roast uncovered for a further 10 minutes – the peaches should be soft, slightly sticky and a rich caramel colour. Allow to cool to room temperature, then cover and refrigerate until well chilled.

Shortbread

Shortbread is made using just four ingredients – butter, sugar, flour and vanilla extract – and the secret lies in the quality of these ingredients. Buy very good unsalted butter and the best vanilla extract you can afford. Delicate and buttery, crumbly and light, shortbread is delectable served alongside poached or roasted fruit, or vanilla ice cream. But arguably, nothing surpasses the pleasure of nibbling on shortbread in the late afternoon with a good pot of tea.

MAKES 9–12 PIECES

230g unsalted butter, at room temperature

125g caster sugar, plus extra to dust

1 tsp vanilla extract

500g plain flour (unbleached), plus extra to dust

Preheat the oven to 170°C/Gas 3. Beat the butter in a large bowl until pale and creamy. Stir in the sugar and vanilla extract and beat until smooth. Now incorporate the flour, a third at a time, mixing again until the dough is smooth after each addition.

Transfer to a lightly floured surface and flatten to a round, no more than 1cm thick. If you prefer, shape into individual shortbreads, using a biscuit cutter. Chill in the fridge for 30 minutes.

If making a large shortbread – as I'm more inclined to do – mark into pieces with a sharp knife, cutting only 3mm into the surface of the dough. Carefully transfer to a baking tray.

Bake on the middle shelf of the oven for 8–10 minutes until the shortbread is pale golden and buttery. Leave on the baking tray for a minute or two, then transfer to a wire rack. While still warm, dust the surface with sugar and carefully break into pieces along the indentations. Store in an airtight container until needed – the shortbread will keep for up to a week.

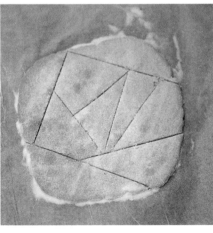

✳ Shortbread should be crisp and light with a melt-in-the-mouth texture. The trick is to handle the dough as little as possible – overworking will make the finished shortbread tough. I mark a whole round roughly into triangular pieces before baking – preferring the appearance of random shapes to neat, uniform pieces.

Sunny flavours

Roasted quail
Roasted red peppers with tomatoes
Grilled aubergine with mint and basil
*
Meringues with strawberries and cream

Roasted quail

Quail is a versatile little bird that cooks quickly and absorbs flavours beautifully. Each bird is a few mouthfuls of succulent breast, followed by tasty leg meat nibbled from the bones. Don't bother with a knife and fork – they prohibit the enjoyment of picking at these tasty small birds. One each is not really enough, so allow two per person. (Illustrated overleaf.)

SERVES 6

12 quail

1 tbsp sea salt

3 tbsp olive oil

Spice mix

2 cardamom pods, seeds extracted

1 tsp cumin seeds

1 tsp coriander seeds

1 tsp fennel seeds

2 star anise

1 dried red chilli, crumbled

If possible, a day ahead, sprinkle the quail lightly all over with the salt, cover loosely and leave in the fridge overnight.

To prepare the spice mix, put all the seeds into a small frying pan with the star anise over a medium heat. Warm through, jiggling the pan once or twice, for about a minute until the seeds begin to jump and pop. Immediately take off the heat. Using a pestle and mortar, grind the toasted spices along with the dried chilli to give a fine-textured spice mix.

Rub the quail all over with the olive oil, then scatter the spice mix evenly over the birds and gently rub into the skin using your fingers. Cover loosely and leave to marinate in a cool place for a couple of hours.

Preheat the oven to 200°C/Gas 6. Heat up a large, dry frying pan over a high heat. Brown the quail in batches, allowing 1 minute on each side and turning once only. It is important that you do not overcrowd the pan, so brown in two or three batches. Place the browned quail in a roasting tin and finish cooking in the oven for 5 minutes. Serve on a warm platter.

Salting the quail lightly before cooking improves their flavour. I also like to marinate them in herbs or – as I have here – a spice mix, which gives them a slightly Middle Eastern flavour.

Roasted red peppers with tomatoes

Slightly smoky, gently sweet, roasted red peppers are a perfect accompaniment to quail. They are also good with soft young goat's curd, black olives, grilled fish or fillet of beef served at room temperature. This recipe calls for the skins to be left on the peppers rather than blistered and removed, as I much prefer them this way. Don't be tempted to use green or yellow peppers, as they won't be as sweet.

SERVES 6

4 large, firm red peppers

2–3 tbsp extra virgin olive oil

1 tbsp red wine vinegar

500g little plum tomatoes

handful of marjoram sprigs, leaves only, chopped

sea salt and freshly ground black pepper

Preheat the oven to 180°C/Gas 4. Using a sharp knife, halve the red peppers lengthways and discard the core and seeds. Now slice each half lengthways into 4 broad strips and place in a bowl.

Pour over a generous glug of olive oil and the wine vinegar. Add the plum tomatoes and half of the chopped marjoram. Season with salt and pepper and toss together well with your hands.

Tip into a baking dish, large enough to hold everything comfortably, and cover loosely with foil. Roast on the middle shelf of the oven for 30 minutes, then uncover and roast for a further 15 minutes, by which time the peppers should be tender but not falling apart.

Allow to cool to room temperature before serving, sprinkled with the remaining chopped marjoram.

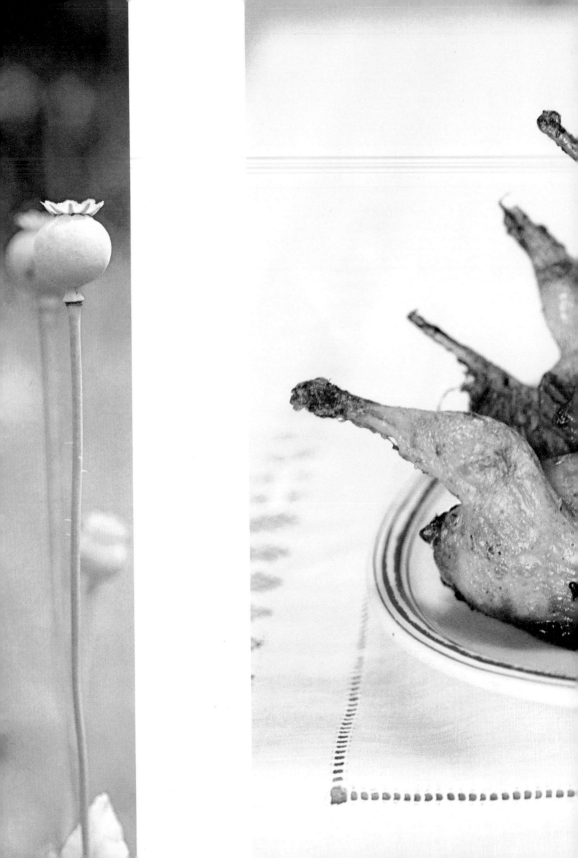

Grilled aubergine with mint and basil

I love the smoky flavour of grilled aubergines and they go so well with the quail in this menu. If possible use the pale purple, fat, round Sicilian variety of aubergine, which has a creamy white top. Otherwise the long, thin purple violetta variety, also from Italy, is similarly thin-skinned with a good, firm texture. If I'm grilling aubergine slices, I rarely bother to salt them first as I consider it unnecessary.

SERVES 6

2 medium aubergines

extra virgin olive oil, for brushing and to drizzle

few squeezes of lemon juice

1 garlic clove, peeled and very finely chopped

handful of basil sprigs, leaves only, roughly torn

few mint sprigs, leaves only, chopped

sea salt and freshly ground pepper

a little aged balsamic vinegar, to drizzle

Cut the aubergines into 3mm slices – either lengthways or into rounds, whichever you prefer. Preheat the grill to medium and brush the aubergine slices on both sides with a little olive oil.

You will probably need to grill the aubergine slices in batches. Lay them on the grill rack and grill for several minutes until well browned on one side before turning to colour the other side. Let them char around the edges slightly – this will impart a lovely smoky flavour. Just make sure you grill the aubergines until they are properly cooked through.

As each batch browns, remove it to a large plate. And, while still hot, drizzle over a little more olive oil, a squeeze of lemon juice, a sprinkling of chopped garlic and a scattering of herbs, then season with salt and pepper. Keep warm in a low oven. Continue in this way until all the aubergine slices are cooked and dressed.

Arrange the warm aubergines on a serving plate and drizzle over a little aged balsamic vinegar just before serving.

Meringues with strawberries and cream

Chewy and delectably sweet, meringues are loved by almost everyone. The best are those that have a crumbly, fragile exterior and a meltingly tender mallowy texture within. Fragrant, homegrown strawberries or raspberries – folded through billowy whipped cream – are the perfect complement. (Also illustrated on page 94.)

SERVES 6

Meringues

4 organic free-range large egg whites, at room temperature

pinch of salt

240g caster sugar

½ tsp vanilla extract

To serve

200ml double cream, at room temperature

1 tbsp icing sugar

250g strawberries, hulled

Preheat the oven to 150°C/Gas 2. Line a large baking tray with baking parchment. Put the egg whites into a large clean, dry bowl with the pinch of salt. Using a balloon whisk, start beating the whites slowly at first, in order to them break down. Once the whites have begun to froth a little, increase your speed and beat until stiff peaks form. Now add the sugar, a spoonful at a time, beating after each addition. Finally whisk in the vanilla extract. You should now have a beautifully shiny, thick meringue.

Spoon the meringue into 6 generous mounds on the baking tray, spacing well apart to allow room for them to expand. Place on the middle shelf of the oven and immediately lower the oven setting to 120°C/Gas ½. Cook for 45 minutes, then turn off the oven and leave the meringues inside to cool completely. If you take them out as soon as they are cooked they are more liable to crack.

When ready to serve, whip the cream with the icing sugar until thick, but still soft. Chop the strawberries into small pieces. Take a third of them and squish with a fork, then combine with the rest. Fold the strawberries through the cream and serve alongside the meringues.

✻ Meringues are not difficult to make, though they are somewhat sensitive – to moisture, fat and sudden change of temperature. Before you start, ensure the bowl and whisk are dry and free from any traces of grease. It is very important to whisk the egg whites thoroughly – to incorporate as much air as possible – until they form stiff peaks, which stand upright without flopping over at all. Continue to whisk thoroughly as you gradually add the sugar – don't be tempted to shower it in too quickly, otherwise the meringue will lose volume. The finished meringue should be smooth, glossy and hold firm peaks on the whisk as you lift it out of the mixture.

Late summer menu

Roasted fillet of beef
Salsa verde
Panzanella
*
Apple and green tomato pie

Roasted fillet of beef

I prefer fillet of beef served warm or at room temperature rather than hot, as I find the extended resting time that this allows makes the meat more tender, and the flavour – generally subtle with fillet – is more pronounced. This is the way I like to cook a whole piece of fillet. Allow 180–200g beef per person. (Illustrated on previous page.)

SERVES 6

1.2kg beef fillet, well trimmed

sea salt and freshly ground black pepper

1 tbsp virgin olive oil

Preheat the oven to 220°C/Gas 7. Place a large heavy-based frying pan over a high heat. Season the meat very generously with salt – this is important for it will give the beef a salty, crisp crust. Sprinkle over some pepper.

When the pan is really hot, add the olive oil and lay the beef fillet in the pan. Brown the meat well all over, but do not move it about too much – just leave it to colour completely on each side before turning. It will take about 10 minutes to brown really well all over.

Once the meat is well browned, transfer it to a roasting tin and place on the middle shelf of the oven. Cook for 12–15 minutes, no longer. Remove to a board and allow to cool for a couple of minutes before wrapping in several layers of foil. Leave to rest in a warm place (near the oven is perfect) for a minimum of 20 minutes if serving warm, or until it has cooled completely.

When ready to serve, unwrap the fillet and cut it into thick slices – 2cm or more. Arrange on a plate, ready to serve with the salsa verde.

Buy beef from animals that have been grass-fed and raised naturally. Beef should be hung for a minimum of 28 days before it is eaten. Look for meat that is dark in colour with fine marbling, and a dry outer skin.

Salsa verde

This fresh-tasting verdant sauce lends a vibrancy to simple grilled and roasted meats. It's the perfect accompaniment to a sumptuous fillet of beef. Serve it in a bowl on the side so guests can help themselves to as much – or as little – as they like. (Illustrated on page 105.)

SERVES 6

bunch of flat-leaf parsley, leaves only

bunch of mint, leaves only

large handful of rocket leaves

1 tbsp Dijon mustard

10 capers, well rinsed

3 good-quality tinned anchovies or from a jar (Ortiz, for example)

2 tbsp red wine vinegar

180ml good-quality olive oil

sea salt

Put the parsley, mint and rocket into a blender along with the mustard, capers and anchovies. Add the wine vinegar and blitz until the herbs are well chopped, but still retain some texture.

With the motor running, slowly pour in the olive oil through the funnel, blending until you have a sludgy green sauce. Taste and season with a little salt only if needed – the anchovies and capers may provide sufficient. Pour into a serving bowl.

Panzanella

Little more than torn stale bread, ripe tomatoes, cucumber and torn basil, this Tuscan salad is surprisingly good. A dressing of verdant green extra virgin olive oil and red wine vinegar, plus a hint of garlic, melds the flavours beautifully. I have seen other ingredients added – finely sliced onion, capers and black olives, for example – but I prefer this simple combination. Grilling the bread and lightly roasting the tomatoes may not be authentic, but I think it enhances the flavour; it also enables the salad to hold up for a little longer.

SERVES 6

16–18 little ripe tomatoes, such as San Marzano

7 tbsp extra virgin olive oil

sea salt and freshly ground black pepper

4 little cucumbers (or ⅔ standard one)

6 thick slices of crusty peasant-style bread

1 garlic clove, peeled and halved

2 tbsp good-quality red wine vinegar

bunch of basil, leaves only

Preheat the oven to 170°C/Gas 3. Wash the tomatoes and pat dry. Pierce each once or twice, using a small sharp knife, then place on a baking tray. Drizzle with 1 tbsp olive oil and season with salt and pepper. Roast for 15 minutes until softened and then allow to cool. (You can skip this stage if you like and simply use the tomatoes fresh.)

Meanwhile, cut the cucumbers into chunks. Grill the bread on both sides until lightly toasted, then rub with the cut garlic clove and drizzle with 1 tbsp olive oil. Season lightly with salt and tear the bread into chunks.

Place the tomatoes, cucumber and bread in a serving bowl and toss lightly. Drizzle over the wine vinegar and the rest of the olive oil, tear in the basil and toss together well with your fingers. Taste for seasoning, adding a grinding of pepper and a little salt if needed. Serve alongside the beef.

The filling for any pie should be generous as this helps to create the lovely undulating top once the pastry lid is on and the pie is baked. The easiest way to apply the pastry lid is to lift the pastry round onto the rolling pin and loosely roll it around the pin, then unravel the pastry over the top of the pie.

Apple and green tomato pie

Unusual as this combination of ingredients sounds, it actually works very well. After all, there is a natural synergy as the fruit are in season at the same time and it's a good way to use up those few tomatoes that never seem to ripen in the garden. Green tomatoes are sharp and firm, as are the first apples of the season – whatever their variety. They do, however, need the right proportion of sugar to tickle out their flavour. The addition of cinnamon gives the pie a lovely cosy feel.

SERVES 6

Pastry

500g plain flour, plus extra to dust

pinch of sea salt

300g unsalted butter, well chilled, cut into cubes

25g caster sugar, plus extra to sprinkle

1 tsp vanilla extract

1 organic free-range large egg yolk

2–3 tbsp cool water

a little milk, to brush

Filling

5 Cox's apples

4 green tomatoes

120g caster sugar

grated zest and juice of 1 lemon

½ tsp ground cinnamon

1 tbsp brown sugar

To make the pastry, sift the flour and salt into a bowl and rub in the butter lightly and evenly until the mixture resembles breadcrumbs. Stir in the sugar and vanilla extract. Lightly beat the egg yolk with the water, then sprinkle over the flour. Work gently with your fingertips to incorporate and form a dough, adding a little more water if needed. Form into a ball and knead lightly on a floured surface. Wrap in cling film and chill for 1 hour.

For the filling, halve the apples and remove the cores, but don't bother to peel them as the skins add texture and flavour. Slice the apples finely into half-moons, slice the tomatoes into rounds and place both in a bowl. Sprinkle with the caster sugar, lemon zest and juice. Set aside while you roll out the pastry.

Divide the pastry in half. Re-wrap one half and return to the fridge. Roll out the other half thinly on a floured surface to a round, 3mm thick and large enough to line the base and sides of a 20cm fluted pie tin. Lift into the tin and press the pastry well into the fluted edge, being careful not to stretch it. Using a sharp knife, cut away the excess pastry so that it is level with the top of the pie tin. Prick the base lightly all over with a fork and chill for 30 minutes. Meanwhile, preheat the oven to 180°C/Gas 4.

Line the pastry case with a piece of baking parchment and half-fill with baking beans (or dried beans). Bake the pastry case on the middle shelf of the oven for 15 minutes, then remove the paper and beans and bake for a further 5 minutes to slightly dry out the base. Set aside to cool a little.

In the meantime, roll out the other piece of pastry thinly to a round, 5mm thick, for the pie lid.

Stir the cinnamon and brown sugar into the filling and spoon into the part-baked pastry case. Using the rolling pin (see left), lift the pastry lid over the top of the pie. Press the pastry edges to seal with your thumbs, fluting them as you do so. Mark a little cross in the centre with a sharp knife and brush with a little milk. Bake on the middle shelf of the oven for 30 minutes, or until the pastry is golden brown.

Place the pie on a wire rack and sprinkle with caster sugar. Leave to stand for 5 minutes, then serve with chilled pouring cream... the contrast of warm pie and cold cream is irresistible.

Afternoon tea

These days, afternoon tea feels like an indulgence – a special opportunity to relax and enjoy luxurious food over gentle conversation with time to spare... so very rare these days. I especially love the idea of an occasion dedicated to all things sweet and delicate – my preferred time to eat sweet food is in the afternoon, rather than at the end of an evening meal. And of course it is lovely to have something savoury as well – nothing too strong in flavour – just enough to counterbalance the sweet things you will be eating.

More often than not, afternoon tea is a simple affair – a tempting home-made cake or scones, or a selection of these, with a pot of tea. But this is also a lovely time of the day to entertain, so I've provided a few menus to encourage you to do so. Of course, you can mix and match the suggestions as you like... and according to the seasons.

Strawberry sponge cake

Somehow this cake manages to be timeless yet charmingly old fashioned at the same time. With its delicate pink icing, it is beautiful to behold on a table laden with other teatime treats.

MAKES 8–10 SLICES

10g butter, melted, plus extra to grease

240g self-raising flour, plus extra to dust

5 organic free-range large eggs, separated

275g caster sugar, plus extra to dust

5 tbsp warm water

small pinch of sea salt

Icing

100g perfectly ripe English strawberries, hulled

120g icing sugar

25g unsalted butter, softened

finely grated zest of 1 orange

Filling

250g strawberries, hulled (except for a few, to finish)

200ml double cream, at room temperature

Preheat the oven to 180°C/Gas 4. Line two 23cm round cake tins with baking parchment, brush the parchment and sides of the tins lightly with melted butter, then dust with a little flour.

Whisk the egg yolks and sugar together in a large bowl until pale and almost doubled in volume; this may take around 10 minutes, so be patient. Fold in the warm water. Sift the flour over the mixture and gradually fold in, using a large metal spoon or spatula.

Now whisk the egg whites in a clean bowl with the pinch of salt until soft peaks form. Carefully fold into the sponge mixture, a third at a time. Finally, gently fold in the melted butter.

Divide the mixture evenly between the prepared cake tins. Bake on the middle shelf of the oven for 20 minutes, or until each cake has slightly shrunk away from the edge of the tin and it springs back when lightly pressed in the centre. Turn out carefully and cool on a wire rack.

To make the icing, purée the strawberries in a blender until smooth, then strain through a fine sieve into a bowl. Add the icing sugar, butter and orange zest to the blender (there's no need to rinse it first) and blend until pale and creamy. Now add the puréed strawberries and process briefly to a beautifully coloured icing. Transfer to a bowl and set aside.

For the filling, slice the strawberries lengthways. Whip the cream until thick, then spread over one sponge cake. Layer the strawberries on top, then cover with the second sponge. Spread the pale pink icing over the surface of the cake, using a palette knife. Halve the reserved strawberries, arrange on top of the cake and dust lightly with caster sugar to finish.

The lightness of a sponge cake is determined by a number of factors. Firstly, the eggs should be organic and as absolutely fresh as possible: fresh eggs encourage a cake to rise well, creating a light texture. Secondly, you need to incorporate as much air into the eggs as possible: the egg yolks and sugar must be beaten together initially until they are pale in colour and substantially increased in volume; the mixture should be thick enough to leave a ribbon trail when the beaters are lifted. Egg whites are similarly whisked to take in as much air as possible. Thirdly, all sponge cakes should be baked as soon as they are mixed. Finally, to check if your cake is ready, look for shrinkage around the sides and press the centre lightly with your fingertips – once cooked it should bounce back.

Lemon and poppy seed cake

This is a good cake to have up your sleeve, perfect for any time of day – I once ate it for breakfast.
Soft and creamy in feel, the poppy seeds provide a slight crunch for a pleasing contrast in texture.

MAKES 6–8 SLICES

115g unsalted butter,
at room temperature,
plus a little melted
butter to grease

275g plain white flour,
plus extra to dust

175g caster sugar

finely grated zest of
3 unwaxed lemons

1 tsp vanilla extract

35g poppy seeds

2½ tsp baking powder

230ml whole milk

4 organic free-range
large egg whites

Icing

2–3 tbsp lemon juice

300g icing sugar

To finish

finely pared zest of
1–2 lemons

Preheat the oven to 170°C/Gas 3. Line a loaf tin, approximately 20 x 11cm, with baking parchment, brush the parchment and sides of the tin lightly with melted butter, then dust with a little flour.

Cream the butter and sugar together, using a hand-held electric mixer, until pale and smooth. Add the lemon zest, vanilla extract and poppy seeds, and sift the flour and baking powder together over the mixture. Stir once or twice, then pour in the milk and stir briefly again – you should have a smooth, homogenised batter.

Whisk the egg whites in a clean, separate bowl until soft peaks form. Fold a third into the cake mixture, using a large metal spoon, then carefully follow in the rest.

Spoon the mixture into the prepared tin and bake for 1¼ hours, or until a skewer inserted into the middle comes out clean. Leave in the tin for a few minutes before turning out onto a wire rack to cool.

To make the icing, warm the lemon juice in a small saucepan, add the icing sugar and stir until smooth. Pour the icing over the cake, spread to cover the top and allow it to drizzle down the sides. Scatter the lemon zest over the surface, to cover generously.

Leave the cake to stand for about 15 minutes before cutting, to allow the icing to set.

Orange and currant scones

This is really one big scone, which you tear into sections and eat warm. In character, it's more like a wholesome, sweet, fruity bread than the more familiar individual golden scones. Flavoured with orange zest and sweet currants, these scone wedges need nothing more than a smear of salty butter.

MAKES 6–8 WEDGES

500g plain white flour, plus extra to dust

1 tsp bicarbonate of soda

½ tsp salt

35g caster sugar

55g cold unsalted butter, cut into pieces

finely grated zest of 3 oranges

250g currants

1 organic free-range large egg, lightly beaten

225–275ml whole milk

Preheat the oven to 200°C/Gas 6. Sift the flour, bicarbonate of soda and salt together into a bowl and stir in the sugar. Rub in the butter, using your fingertips. Then stir in the grated orange zest and currants, using a round-bladed knife.

Make a well in the centre, add the egg and pour in most of the milk. Mix gently to a soft dough, using your hands, adding the extra milk if needed.

Turn out onto a floured surface and shape into a round, using the flat of your hands. Now mark into 6–8 triangles with a sharp knife, cutting no than 3mm into the dough. Place on a baking tray.

Bake on the middle shelf of the oven for 15 minutes, then lower the oven setting to 180°C/Gas 4. Bake for a further 15–20 minutes, or until the scone is golden brown on top and sounds hollow when tapped on the base. Transfer to a wire rack to cool slightly. Serve warm, with butter.

Chocolate cake with cream cheese icing

This cake is sweet, dark and sludgy, with a contrasting American-style icing of whipped cream cheese, icing sugar and butter. It is not the sort of sophisticated smoky rich chocolate cake that you will find on a restaurant menu, but rather one that should be eaten at home. It is best served on its own as a teatime treat – it is too independent to share the stage with anything else. A small slice is all that is needed.

MAKES 8–10 SLICES

150g good-quality dark chocolate (minimum 64% cocoa solids)

185g unsalted butter, at room temperature, plus extra to grease

375g plain flour, plus extra to dust

1 tsp baking powder

185g caster sugar

185g soft brown sugar

3 organic free-range large eggs, at room temperature

185ml whole milk

1 tsp vanilla extract

Icing

300g soft cream cheese

75g unsalted butter, at room temperature

600g icing sugar

To finish

A little dark chocolate, for grating

Preheat the oven to 170°C/Gas 3. Melt the chocolate in a heatproof bowl over a pan of barely simmering water (see below). When it is melted, smooth and glossy, remove from the heat and set aside to cool slightly.

Lightly grease and flour three 20cm sandwich cake tins (or two 25cm cake tins) and line with baking parchment. Sift the flour and baking powder together and set aside.

Using an electric mixer, cream the butter until light and pale – this will take about 3 minutes. Add the caster and brown sugars and cream until light and very fluffy. Add the eggs, one at a time, beating after each addition. Now incorporate the chocolate, mixing until evenly combined.

Finally fold in the flour alternately with the milk and vanilla, using a large metal spoon or spatula. The batter should be smooth and glossy.

Divide the mixture between the prepared cake tins and bake on the middle shelf of the oven for 20 minutes, or until a skewer inserted in the centre comes out clean.

Place the tins on a wire rack and leave to cool for 5 minutes or so, then turn out the cakes onto the rack and leave to cool completely before icing.

For the icing, using an electric mixer, beat all the ingredients together until soft and completely smooth. Spread the icing over the cake while it is still soft. Place in the fridge for an hour or so before serving.

Lay one sponge on a board and spread generously with a third of the icing. Place a second sponge on top and spread with another third of the icing. Position the final sponge on top and cover with the rest of the icing. Grate a little dark chocolate over the top to serve.

The best way to melt chocolate is in a heatproof bowl set over a pan containing about 5cm gently simmering water (this is called a bain-marie). The bowl should not be in direct contact with the water, otherwise the chocolate is liable to overheat. First break up or chop the chocolate to encourage it to melt evenly. And don't stir it during melting, as this can dull the shine.

Classic English midsummer tea

Cucumber sandwiches
Blackberry and raspberry trifle
Lemon verbena tea

Cucumber sandwiches

There is nothing more dainty or elegant than cucumber sandwiches served on the freshest bread imaginable – sliced thinly, with the crusts removed. A sprinkling of poppy seeds is the perfect finishing touch. Serve the sandwiches piled carefully on the prettiest plate you can find.

MAKES 24

2 medium cucumbers

1 tsp sea salt

2 tbsp unsalted butter, softened

2 tbsp home-made mayonnaise (see page 81), optional

12 thin slices of bread

1 tsp poppy seeds

Peel the cucumbers, cut in half lengthways and scoop out the seeds, using a teaspoon. Now slice the cucumbers into paper-thin slices and sprinkle lightly with the salt. Place in a colander over a bowl and refrigerate for an hour or so, to allow the cucumbers to drain.

Beat the butter in a bowl until pale and soft. For a slightly richer flavour, beat in the mayonnaise. Spread on one side of the bread slices.

Squeeze the cucumbers in a tea towel to remove any excess liquid. Arrange the cucumber slices on half of the buttered bread slices and sandwich together with the rest of the bread.

Now sprinkle with the poppy seeds. Using a sharp bread knife, cut off the bread crusts. Slice each sandwich lengthways into four and arrange on a serving plate.

At the height of summer, a traditional English afternoon tea wouldn't be complete without little cucumber sandwiches, and a fresh berry trifle makes a spectacular centrepiece. I've kept this menu very simple, but you can always add to it if you like, perhaps serving a tempting Strawberry sponge cake (see page 114).

Blackberry and raspberry trifle

Distinctly old fashioned and decadent in feel, this is a proper trifle. Luscious layers of sponge, custard, cream and fruit all meld together in this most classic of English desserts. Everything is made from scratch, but the end result is well worth the time and effort. You can cheat if you're short of time, using a good-quality shop-bought sponge, perhaps even a tub of ready-made 'fresh' custard. It will still be good, but you'll be denied the full satisfaction of making a glorious trifle. (Illustrated on page 120.)

SERVES 8–10

Sponge

100g unsalted butter, softened, plus a little melted butter to grease

100g self-raising flour, plus extra to dust

100g caster sugar

2 organic free-range large eggs

1 tsp baking powder

small pinch of salt

1 tsp vanilla extract

Custard

150ml double cream

300ml whole milk

8 organic free-range large egg yolks

80g caster sugar

75g plain flour

1 tsp vanilla extract

Fruit

300g blackberries

300g raspberries

150g caster sugar

finely grated zest of 1 orange

To finish

450ml double cream

50g almonds, toasted and chopped

handful each of raspberries and blackberries

icing sugar, to dust

For the sponge, preheat the oven to 180°C/Gas 4. Line two 18cm round cake tins with baking parchment, brush the parchment and sides of the tins lightly with melted butter, then dust with a little flour.

Beat the butter and sugar together, using a hand-held electric mixer, until pale and soft, then beat in the eggs one at a time. Sift the flour, baking powder and salt together over the mixture and fold in, using a large metal spoon. Finally fold in the vanilla extract.

Divide the mixture between the prepared tins and bake on the middle shelf of the oven for 20 minutes, or until the cakes are springy to the touch and have shrunk back slightly from the sides of the tins. Leave in the tins for 5 minutes before turning out onto a wire rack to cool.

To make the custard, pour the cream and milk into a saucepan and bring to a simmer, then remove from the heat. Beat the egg yolks, sugar and flour together in a large bowl until pale and thick, then add the vanilla extract and slowly pour in the warm, creamy milk, whisking as you do so. Return the custard to the pan and stir constantly over the lowest possible heat with a wooden spoon, until the custard begins to thicken; don't let it boil. The custard is ready when it is thick enough to lightly coat the back of the spoon. Immediately pour into a bowl and allow to cool; it will continue to thicken as it cools.

Meanwhile, tip the berries and sugar into a saucepan and cook over a medium-low heat for 5 minutes, or until the sugar has dissolved and the fruit begins to soften and bleed. Stir in the orange zest. Set aside to cool.

To assemble the trifle, cut one sponge into slices and use to line the base of a large, glass serving bowl, cutting smaller pieces to fill the gaps as necessary. Spoon over half the fruit, followed by half of the custard. Whip the cream until soft peaks form, then spread a layer over the custard. Repeat these layers, finishing with a top layer of cream, then sprinkle with the chopped toasted almonds. Arrange a border of fresh berries around the edge of the trifle.

Leave the trifle to stand in the fridge for an hour or two before serving, dusted lightly with icing sugar.

Lemon verbena tea

Tea made with fresh herbs from the garden has a delicacy that is quite beautiful. The flavour is clean and clear, pure and ethereal. Like mint, lemon verbena grows in abundance from early spring through to autumn and I have both herbs in my garden at home. I often cut stems of verbena to place in a vase in my kitchen, encouraging its lemony scent to fill the air.

MAKES 600ML

5 lemon verbena sprigs

1 tbsp granulated sugar (optional)

600ml boiling water

Place the sprigs of verbena in a heatproof glass jug or teapot. Add the sugar if using – it will enhance the herby flavour, but isn't essential.

Now pour on the boiling water, stir to dissolve the sugar and leave to infuse for 5 minutes before serving.

Fresh herb tea makes a wonderful change from traditional teas, such as Earl Grey or Assam, and its freshness offsets the sweet indulgence of this spread perfectly. As an alternative to lemon verbena, use a generous bunch of mint, steeping it in boiling water, with a little sugar if you like, as above.

Elegant and easy afternoon tea

Little chicken
and watercress sandwiches

Lemon sorbet with crushed mint

Ricotta cheesecake

Roasted rhubarb

Little chicken and watercress sandwiches

This combination of succulent chicken, peppery watercress and creamy mayonnaise works beautifully as a delicate teatime sandwich filling.

MAKES 24

250g cooked chicken breast (poached or roasted), skinned

about 5 tbsp home-made mayonnaise (see page 81)

small bunch of watercress, leaves only

sea salt and freshly ground black pepper

few gratings of fresh nutmeg, to taste

5 tbsp unsalted butter, softened

12 slices of thin very fresh white bread

Finely chop the chicken and place in a bowl with the mayonnaise.

Set aside a small handful of watercress leaves for garnish. Chop the rest of the watercress finely and add to the chicken. Mix well and season with salt, pepper and nutmeg to taste.

Lightly butter the bread slices on one side. Spread the chicken mixture on half of the buttered bread slices. Cover with the remaining bread slices and press down lightly with the palm of your hand.

Using a sharp bread knife, cut off the crusts. Slice each sandwich lengthways into four and arrange on a serving plate. Garnish with the reserved watercress.

Lemon sorbet with crushed mint

This is a lovely palate cleanser between little savoury sandwiches and a slice of cake or two. Mint leaves are crushed into sugar to make an unusual topping for the lemon sorbet. I find the sweet, fresh mintiness of the topping works so well with the sharp, tart flavour of the sorbet.

SERVES 8–10

4 lemons

500g caster sugar

1 litre fresh lemon juice

small pinch of salt

1 tbsp limoncello liqueur (optional)

Mint crush

bunch of mint, leaves only

2 tbsp caster sugar

finely grated zest of 2 lemons

Quarter the lemons and remove the pips, then place in a food processor with the sugar. Pulse until you have a coarse-textured mixture with little pieces of lemon peel still running through. Tip into a large bowl and stir in the lemon juice, salt and liqueur if using.

Churn the mixture in an ice-cream maker until frozen, then transfer to a suitable container and place in the freezer.

To make the mint crush, pound the mint leaves and sugar together, using a pestle and mortar, then stir in the lemon zest.

Remove the sorbet from the freezer 10 minutes before you wish to serve it, to allow it to soften slightly. Spoon into chilled little glasses and spoon the mint crush on top. Serve immediately.

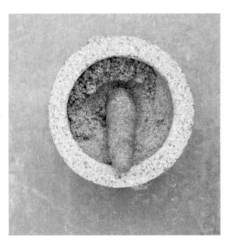

For the mint topping, use a pestle and mortar to pound the mint leaves and sugar together to break down the mint leaves to release their fragrance and pulverise the sugar crystals.

Ricotta cheesecake

This cheesecake has a hint of southern Italy about it, where the combination of ricotta and candied peel is popular. Incredibly simple to make, it doesn't require any baking skills, just good ingredients. Exact quantities are not imperative and you can add almost any flavourings you like. Also, you can make it ahead and keep it in the fridge for a couple of days. It can be eaten just as it is, but I like to serve it with roasted rhubarb, caramelised oranges (see page 164), or a fruit compote, such as apricot (see page 136).

MAKES 10 SLICES

2 tbsp sultanas

2 tbsp Pedro Ximénez sherry

1 tbsp warm water

500g ricotta cheese

250g mascarpone

150g icing sugar

4 organic free-range large eggs

finely grated zest of 1 orange

finely grated zest of 1 lemon

4 tbsp candied peel, chopped

60g pine nuts

Preheat the oven to 170°C/Gas 3. Put the sultanas in a bowl, add the sherry and warm water and leave to soak for 10 minutes to plump up.

Line the base and sides of a loose-bottomed 23cm round cake tin with baking parchment.

Place the ricotta and mascarpone in a large bowl, sift in the icing sugar and beat well to combine. Beat in the eggs, one by one.

Drain the sultanas and add to the mixture with the orange and lemon zests, candied peel and half of the pine nuts. Stir once again to distribute the ingredients evenly.

Pour the mixture into the prepared tin and scatter the remaining pine nuts over the surface. Bake on the middle shelf of the oven for 50 minutes to 1 hour until the cheesecake feels lightly firm on top when gently pressed in the middle. Leave to cool in the tin, then chill before serving.

Carefully unmould the cheesecake onto a large plate and accompany with the roasted rhubarb if serving.

Roasted rhubarb

A little pot of soft fresh fruit compote is nice at teatime – spooned onto the ricotta cheesecake, or pound cake (see page 136) or scones, for example. Rhubarb is available during the spring and early summer, but my favourite is the beautiful pale and less sharp winter-forced rhubarb. Roasting the stems lends a slightly caramelised flavour and the fruit retains its shape better. Peach or nectarine slices can be roasted in the same way, though they will need rather less sugar and less time to soften.

SERVES 8–10

6 sticks of rhubarb, washed

140g golden caster sugar

thickly pared zest and juice of 1 orange

1 vanilla pod, sliced in half lengthways

Preheat the oven to 180°C/Gas 4. Cut the rhubarb into 5cm lengths and place in a bowl. Sprinkle over the sugar and orange juice and toss well, then tip onto a baking tray and spread out evenly.

Tuck in the vanilla pod and orange zest, cover with foil and bake for 10 minutes, then remove the foil and roast for a further 10 minutes. Discard the vanilla and lemon zest.

Allow to cool before serving. This compote is also very nice served chilled – especially when the weather is a little warmer.

Sweet temptation

Pound cake
Apricot compote
Gooey chocolate and raisin biscuits
Earl Grey sorbet

Pound cake

This gently sweet, dense-textured cake is lovely for its plainness and simplicity. A pot of mild Earl Grey tea is the perfect complement. I also like to serve a fresh fruit compote and a bowl of crème fraîche on the side to redress the sweetness.

MAKES 12 SLICES

450g unsalted butter, softened, plus a little melted butter to grease

450g plain flour, sifted, plus extra to dust

½ tsp sea salt

½ tsp baking powder

½ tsp bicarbonate of soda

450g golden caster sugar

2 tsp vanilla extract

6 organic free-range large eggs

125ml whole milk

finely grated zest of 1 orange

finely grated zest of 1 lemon

Preheat the oven to 160°C/Gas 3. Line a loose-bottomed 23cm round cake tin with foil and baking parchment, brush the parchment and sides of the tin lightly with melted butter, then dust with a little flour.

Sift the flour, salt, baking powder and bicarbonate of soda together into a bowl and set aside.

Using an electric mixer, beat the butter, sugar and vanilla extract together on a low speed for 2 minutes, then increase the speed to high and beat until pale and fluffy. Turn the speed to low again and beat in the eggs, one at a time, alternately with the milk.

Using a large metal spoon, fold the flour into the mixture in three batches, followed by the orange and lemon zest, until evenly combined.

Spoon the cake mixture into the prepared cake tin and gently level the surface with the back of the spoon. Stand the cake tin on a baking sheet on the middle shelf of the oven and bake for 1¼ hours, or until the cake has begun to shrink away from the sides of the tin and a skewer inserted into the centre comes out clean.

Leave in the tin for 5 minutes, then turn out onto a wire rack. This cake is at its best eaten still slightly warm from the oven.

Apricot compote

This simple compote is the perfect accompaniment to a sweet, dense cake, such as the one above, or an almond or polenta cake. You can also stir it into thick Greek yoghurt to have at breakfast, or after lunch or supper. The apricot is a distant relative of the almond tree – add a few of the apricot stones to the bubbling fruit and they will impart a lovely hint of bitter almonds.

SERVES 10–12

1kg ripe apricots

175g caster sugar

pared zest of 1 lemon

1 vanilla pod, split in half lengthways

tiny pinch of salt

Using a small sharp knife, halve the apricots lengthways and remove the stones; reserve 3 or 4 stones and discard the rest.

Put the apricots into a saucepan and add the sugar, lemon zest, vanilla pod, salt and reserved apricot stones. Pour in a little water, just enough to give a 1cm depth, and place over a low heat. Once the sugar has dissolved, increase the heat to medium-high and cook, stirring from time to time, for 10 minutes. The apricots should be soft and brighter in colour, their skins having slipped off. Set aside to cool.

Spoon the cooled compote into a suitable container, cover and refrigerate until well chilled. It will keep well in the fridge for 3–4 days.

Gooey chocolate and raisin biscuits

Biscuits are really not difficult to make and the effort is always appreciated. I like chocolate biscuits to be soft and gooey – almost sticky – and I prefer to eat them still just a little warm. As they emerge from the oven, the smell is irresistible – enough to make anyone hungry. You'll find it difficult to eat just one...

MAKES ABOUT 30

100g plain flour

¼ tsp baking powder

good pinch of salt

200g unsalted butter

135g soft brown sugar

25g caster sugar

1 vanilla pod, split lengthways

1 organic free-range large egg

3 tsp milk

90g rolled oats

150g raisins

175g good-quality dark chocolate, chopped

Preheat the oven to 160°C/Gas 3. Line two or three large baking trays with baking parchment. Sift the flour, baking powder and salt together into a bowl and set aside.

Using an electric mixer, beat the butter and both sugars together until well combined. Scrape in the seeds from the vanilla pod and continue to beat until pale and thick. Now beat in the egg and milk, followed by the flour mixture.

Finally fold in the oats, raisins and chopped chocolate, using a large metal spoon or spatula.

Spoon the dough into mounds on the prepared baking trays, making sure that they are evenly spaced and well apart to allow room for spreading. Bake in the oven for 15 minutes until golden.

Leave the biscuits on the trays for a few minutes to firm up, then transfer to a wire rack to cool. Serve still slightly warm.

Earl Grey sorbet

This is really just iced tea, but cooler, very refreshing and a lovely end to afternoon tea on a warm summer's day. It needs to be eaten slowly with small spoons, so the icy coolness slips easily down your throat, gently cleaning your palate at the same time. There should be no more than a whisper of the flavour of the tea, otherwise the taste may be overpowering.

SERVES 8–10

400g caster sugar

1 litre water

2 vanilla pods, split in half lengthways

1½ tbsp Earl Grey loose-leaf tea

Put the sugar and water into a saucepan along with the vanilla pods. Bring to the boil over a medium heat, stirring once or twice until the sugar has dissolved, then turn down the heat slightly and cook until the syrup has thickened and become a little viscous.

Tip the tea leaves into a large bowl, then pour on the hot vanilla-flavoured sugar syrup. Stir to combine and set aside to infuse until cool.

Strain the mixture through a fine sieve into an ice-cream maker and churn, according to the manufacturer's instructions until firm, then transfer to a suitable container and place in the freezer.

Remove the sorbet from the freezer 15 minutes before you wish to serve it, to allow it to soften – it should be loose and almost beginning to melt. Scoop into glass dishes and serve immediately.

Simple weekday dinner

Midweek suppers are always casual in our home – simple comforting food to satisfy everyone after a tiring day's work. If we have a dessert, it is likely to be something very straightforward and easy to prepare. One course is often enough, though usually we will have a salad – eaten after the main course rather than with it – right through the year, not just in summer. Leaves carefully dressed should be eaten on their own – to enjoy their particular taste, but equally so as not interfere with the flavours of the primary dish.

Never underestimate the beauty of ripe seasonal fruit to end a meal. In its most perfect incarnation, it cannot be surpassed. One flawless peach, limey fragrant slices of mango, full-flavoured autumn raspberries, or the sweet juice that drips from a slice of watermelon on a warm summer's day – all so enticing and breathtaking in their simplicity.

Midweek special

Grilled steaks
Buttermilk mashed potatoes
Slow-cooked chard
*
Bread and butter pudding

Grilled steaks

At home we are not big meat eaters, but sometimes I am overwhelmed with a craving that cannot be ignored. Thickly sliced well-aged fillet of beef – generously seasoned and cooked to a firm, salty crust on the outside yet meltingly tender and pink within – does the trick. Here I've served it with mashed potato and gently cooked chard. Place a pot of Dijon mustard on the table for those who wish to smear some onto their steak. This menu is easily adjusted to accommodate the number around the table. (Illustrated on previous page.)

SERVES 6

6 thick fillet steaks, about 200g each

2 tsp sea salt

1 tsp freshly ground black pepper

1 tbsp mild-tasting olive oil

Season the meat really well on both sides with the salt and pepper; the salt should form a loose crust. Place a heavy-based non-stick pan over a medium-high heat, add the olive oil and allow it to become really hot.

When the oil is almost smoking, lay the steaks in the pan, spacing them well apart, and turn down the heat very slightly. Allow to sizzle undisturbed for 3 minutes, then turn and cook on the other side for a further 3–4 minutes according to taste.

Transfer the steaks to a warm plate and leave to rest in a warm place for 10 minutes before serving.

Fillet steak is an expensive rare treat, so make sure your butcher gives you a really good well-aged piece. Look for meat that is dark red in colour, with a light, even marbling of creamy fat through the flesh.

Buttermilk mashed potatoes

The best mash of all is as smooth as silk and just a little buttery. Plenty of freshly ground black pepper is essential. Buttermilk gives this mash a slightly sharp, pleasant taste, which is underpinned by the grated Parmesan. Both Cyprus and Desirée are good varieties of potato for mashing. I generally allow one medium potato per person. (Illustrated on page 143.)

SERVES 6

6 medium potatoes, peeled and washed

sea salt and freshly ground black pepper

50g unsalted butter

180–200ml buttermilk or crème fraîche

50g Parmesan cheese, freshly grated

Cut the potatoes into small even-sized pieces and place in a saucepan containing enough cold water to cover them. Add 1½ tsp salt. Bring to the boil over a medium heat, then turn down the heat, put the lid on and simmer for 15–20 minutes until the potatoes are really tender. The water will become cloudy and the potatoes should literally crumble and fall apart when pierced with a fork. Drain the potatoes and set aside.

Add the butter and 180ml buttermilk or crème fraîche to the pan (in which the potatoes were cooked), then place over a low heat until the butter is melted and the milk is almost at a simmer. Take off the heat.

Return the potatoes to the pan and mash thoroughly, using a hand-held potato masher, until really smooth. You may add a little more buttermilk if the mash feels a little firm, but it must be warmed through before adding. Stir in the Parmesan and season with plenty of pepper.

Serve piping hot – this is a must. (If not serving at once, you can reheat the mash carefully over a low heat, stirring to avoid it catching and burning on the bottom, which gives an unpleasant smoky flavour.)

The secret to any good vegetable purée is to add liquid that is just below boiling point; adding cold liquid will only result in a lumpy finish.

Slow-cooked chard

I love to serve this side dish with grilled or pan-fried meat or game. Cooked slowly in olive oil, the chard leaves turn inky black, contrasting the creamy stalks beautifully.

SERVES 6

2 bunches of Swiss chard

sea salt and freshly ground black pepper

3 tbsp extra virgin olive oil

Put a large saucepan of well-salted water on to boil. Wash the chard well under cold running water and shake off the excess, then cut the leaves from the stalks and put the leaves to one side. Cut the chard stalks into short lengths.

Once the water is boiling, plunge in the stalks and cook for 3 minutes. Remove with a slotted spoon and drain in a colander. Now add the leaves to the boiling water (in which the stalks were cooked) and cook for 1 minute, then drain thoroughly. Chop the leaves when they are cool enough to handle.

Place a clean, dry saucepan on a low heat and add the olive oil. Once the oil is warm, add all of the chard with a good pinch of salt. Put the lid on and cook gently for 30 minutes until very soft, stirring from time to time. Taste for seasoning, adding a little more salt if necessary; a good grinding of pepper is essential. Serve hot.

✿ Chard stalks and leaves have different cooking times, so they need to be boiled separately. To prepare, lay the chard on a board and slice down either side of the creamy white stalk, using a small sharp knife, to separate the dark leaves. Slice the stalks across into short lengths.

Bread and butter pudding

This much-loved pudding is pure comfort food – a lovely, simple dish to cook for family and friends. I like to serve it warm with a jug of cold thick pouring cream on the side. A spoonful of poached fruit or fruit compote can be good too, though I probably prefer it just swimming in a pool of rich cream. Bread with a little bite works best – French or Italian – not the ubiquitous soft, sliced bread you can buy from supermarkets.

SERVES 6

6–8 slices of bread, 2.5cm thick, crusts removed

unsalted butter, softened, for spreading

2 organic free-range medium eggs

5 organic free-range medium egg yolks

125g caster sugar

½ tsp vanilla extract

½ tsp freshly grated nutmeg, or to taste

300ml whole milk

200ml double cream

100g sugar cubes, crushed

Preheat the oven to 180°C/Gas 4. Lightly spread the bread slices on one side with butter. In a bowl, beat the whole eggs, egg yolks, caster sugar, vanilla extract and grated nutmeg together really well.

Pour the milk and cream into a pan and bring almost to a simmer, then slowly pour onto the egg mixture, whisking as you do so. Whisk until thoroughly combined, then pour through a sieve into a medium rectangular baking dish.

Float the buttered bread on top of the custard, making sure that the buttered side is facing upwards. Sprinkle over the crushed sugar cubes.

Stand the baking dish in a roasting tin and pour in enough hot water to come halfway up the side of the dish. Cook on the middle shelf of the oven for 45 minutes, or until a sharp knife inserted into the centre of the pudding comes out clean.

Remove the baking dish from the bain-marie and leave to stand for 5–10 minutes to cool slightly. Serve straight from the dish.

More often than not, I suggest you position dishes on the middle shelf of the oven – where the temperature is most even. The top shelf is often too hot, while the bottom shelf is generally cooler than the temperature indicated on your dial. Never place food directly on the floor of the oven – it will be ruined. Instead stand it on a rack to allow air to circulate below.

Peasant-style supper

Chicken with rice and basil
Buttered spinach (see page 164)
Little glazed carrots
*
Cheese or seasonal fruit

*I love this effortless meal. It would be good
to finish with a fairly soft, mild cheese, perhaps
taleggio, or a semi-hard cows milk such as toma.
Or you might prefer fruit – one perfectly ripe
peach at the height of summer, a pear in the
autumn, or clementines in winter.*

Chicken with rice and basil

This was one of the first things I learnt to cook away from home. I was just eighteen and living in Florence. My friend Gabrielle took me to the market, where we bought a chicken and a large bunch of basil. Once back at her flat she proceeded to teach me this most simple of meals. I have continued to cook it over the years – for me it is very nurturing and nostalgic. (Illustrated on previous page.)

SERVES 6

1 organic free-range chicken, about 1.6kg, jointed into 6 pieces

sea salt and freshly ground black pepper

2 tbsp olive oil

1 red onion, peeled and finely sliced

2 garlic cloves, peeled and crushed

1 dried red chilli

100g risotto rice (Arborio or Carnaroli)

750ml dry white wine

large bunch of basil

extra virgin olive oil, to drizzle

Season the chicken joints well all over with salt and pepper. Place a large flameproof casserole over a medium heat and add the olive oil. Once the oil is sizzling, brown the chicken pieces in batches, skin side down, without turning, until they are golden brown; this will take about 5 minutes. Set aside on a plate.

Pour off any excess fat, leaving a little in the casserole. Lower the heat, add the onion and sweat gently for about 10 minutes until soft and translucent. Now add the garlic and crumble in the dried chilli. Stir once or twice, then tip in the rice and toss it through.

Now increase the heat slightly, pour in the wine and return the chicken to the pot. Put the lid on, turn the heat to low and cook for 20 minutes. By this time the chicken should be cooked through and the rice will have a gentle bite.

Tear the basil with your fingers and scatter over the chicken. Stir through, then taste and adjust the seasoning if necessary; it will almost certainly need more salt.

Serve in warm soup plates, drizzled with a little extra virgin olive oil. Buttered spinach and little glazed carrots are nice accompaniments.

In a classic risotto, the rice is fed slowly, ladle by ladle with simmering liquor – usually stock – until it is just cooked. Here I have added only wine – cold and in one go. This way, the rice takes on the flavour of the wine quite profoundly and the addition of roughly torn basil at the end is a good complement to the flavour.

Little glazed carrots

Perfect with almost anything, these soft, sweet carrots are just the thing to accompany a simple supper in the autumn when they come into their own. Choose small carrots that are free from blemishes and feel heavy for their size.

SERVES 6

500g small sweet carrots, peeled and trimmed

25g butter

2 tsp honey

small bunch of thyme

sea salt

handful of flat-leaf parsley, leaves only, finely chopped

Scrub or peel the carrots and trim them, leaving on a little of the green leafy tufts. Place in a saucepan with the butter and honey. Pour on enough cold water to just cover the carrots and add the thyme and a good pinch of salt. Bring just to the boil, then turn down the heat to a simmer and cook until just tender; this will take about 10 minutes. Discard the thyme.

Now turn up the heat and boil rapidly until all the water has evaporated and the carrots are coated in a lovely shiny glaze.

Serve warm, with a generous sprinkling of chopped parsley.

Slow-cook magic

Shoulder of lamb with
sweet paprika and chickpeas

Slow-cooked courgettes with mint

*

Rice pudding with poached prunes

Shoulder of lamb with sweet paprika and chickpeas

Slow cooking is a lovely, heartwarming and satisfying way to cook. It allows time for flavours to develop and meld together and more often than not I find the end result exceeds my expectations. In essence, this is a one-pot meal. The only accompaniment you will need is a green vegetable, such as slow-cooked courgettes, or a lightly dressed salad of seasonal leaves. (Also illustrated on previous page.)

SERVES 4–6

1.5kg shoulder of lamb joint

sea salt and freshly ground black pepper

3 tbsp olive oil

1½ tsp fennel seeds

750ml dry white wine

2 red onions, peeled and chopped

5 garlic cloves, peeled and roughly crushed

small bunch of thyme

1 dried red chilli

1 tsp sweet Spanish paprika

2 red peppers

250g good-quality tinned plum tomatoes or from a jar

250g cooked chickpeas (tinned ones can be used)

Preheat the oven to 180°C/Gas 4. Trim the lamb of all fat and season generously all over with salt and pepper. Place a large, sturdy roasting tin on the hob over a medium heat and add 1 tbsp olive oil. When it is hot, add the lamb and brown well all over; this will take 10 minutes or so.

Meanwhile, put the fennel seeds into a small frying pan over a high heat and warm for a minute, or until they begin to pop and release their aroma. Immediately take off the heat and pound, using a pestle and mortar. Set aside.

Once the lamb is golden brown, remove it from the roasting tin and set aside. Turn the heat down slightly and deglaze the tin with the wine, stirring to scrape up the sediment. Allow the wine to bubble and reduce by about a third, then pour it off into a jug.

Add the remaining 2 tbsp olive oil to the roasting tin and warm over a low heat. Add the onions, garlic, crushed fennel seeds and thyme and cook gently for 10 minutes until the onions are softened and slightly caramelised. Crumble in the dried chilli, add the paprika and return the lamb to the roasting tin. Pour over the reduced wine and turn off the heat.

Cover the roasting tin tightly with foil and place on the middle shelf of the oven. Allow the lamb to cook, undisturbed, for 2 hours.

Meanwhile, halve and deseed the peppers, then cut each half into 8 pieces. Take the lamb out of the oven, uncover and scatter over the sliced peppers, and tomatoes. Re-cover and return to the oven for a further 1 hour.

Now take out the roasting tin, uncover and stir in the chickpeas. Turn the oven setting up to 200°C/Gas 6 and cook for a final 15 minutes. Discard the thyme. Set aside to rest in a warm place for 20 minutes.

Before serving, tear the meat from the bones – it will come away easily – tongs are the easiest implement to use. Return the meat to the pan and taste for seasoning, adjusting as necessary. Reheat gently to warm through if necessary and serve.

Meat is browned before other ingredients are added for two reasons: firstly to seal in the flavours and secondly to give a much more appealing colour to the finished dish. When browning meat, make sure it has plenty of space in the pan. Use a large pan or roasting tin to brown a whole joint. If you are browning pieces of meat – for a casserole, perhaps – do so in batches if necessary; the meat will stew rather than brown if the pan is overcrowded.

Slow-cooked courgettes with mint

This is one of my favourite ways of cooking this vegetable. With long, slow cooking courgettes take on a new depth of flavour and become so soft they are almost jammy in consistency. A beautiful accompaniment for the lamb, it can also be served either warm or at room temperature drizzled with a little olive oil, alongside white fish such as sea bass or turbot. (Illustrated on previous page.)

SERVES 4–6

1kg courgettes, trimmed

1 tbsp unsalted butter

2 tbsp extra virgin olive oil

3 garlic cloves, peeled and very finely chopped

1 dried red chilli

sea salt

handful of mint leaves, very finely chopped

Slice the courgettes into fine rounds. Put the butter and olive oil into a heavy-based saucepan and heat gently until the butter melts. Add the garlic and crumble in the dried chilli, stir once or twice, then cook for a few minutes until the garlic is soft, but not coloured.

Now add the courgettes with a good pinch of salt and put the lid on the pan. Cook over a low heat for 40 minutes, stirring regularly to ensure that the courgettes do not stick to the bottom of the pan. Once cooked they should be very soft, almost completely fallen apart.

Stir the chopped mint through the courgettes and serve warm, alongside the lamb.

Rice pudding with poached prunes

Sometimes I dream about rice pudding. Properly made, it is sweet, gentle and always alluring to me. And it has the added advantage of taking very little effort. I like to use risotto rice – its small, plump grains absorb the flavours of sweet, vanilla-infused milk better than long- or short-grain rice. You might prefer a dollop of jam with your rice pudding instead of the prunes; if so try infusing the rice during cooking with 3 or 4 rose-scented geranium leaves too.

SERVES 4–6

250g risotto rice

900ml whole milk

1 vanilla pod, split lengthways

peel of 1 lemon

small pinch of salt

150g caster sugar

200ml double cream

Poached prunes

150g plump, soft prunes

4 tbsp Pedro Ximénez sherry

5 tbsp boiling water

Rinse the rice well under cold running water, then tip it into a heavy-based saucepan. Add the milk, vanilla pod, lemon peel and salt and bring almost to a simmer over a medium heat. Now turn down the heat as low as possible (a heat-diffuser mat is useful here) and put the lid on, placing it slightly off centre, so it isn't quite covering the pan. Cook, stirring every now and then, for 20 minutes, or until the rice is cooked but still retains the slightest bite.

In the meantime, stone the prunes and place in a small bowl. Pour over the sherry, followed by the boiling water and leave to steep for 20 minutes.

When the rice is cooked until al dente, stir in the sugar and cream and cook for a further 10 minutes. The pudding needs to be creamy with a soft consistency – it should easily drop from a spoon.

Transfer the rice pudding to a serving dish and allow to stand for 5–10 minutes. Serve warm, not piping hot, topped with the poached prunes.

Winter comfort

Chicken pie
Buttered spinach
*
Caramelised blood oranges

Chicken pie

This is a deeply satisfying weekday supper dish. Lovely on a winter's evening when the light drops from the sky late in the afternoon, it will warm you right to your core. I like to serve the pie simply with a mound of buttered wilted spinach. (Illustrated on previous page.)

You can prepare the pie in advance and keep it in the fridge, ready to glaze and bake – just allow an extra 10 minutes in the oven. Or you might prefer to just make the pastry ahead – wrap well and keep in the fridge for a few days, or in the freezer for a couple of weeks or so. The pie will also reheat successfully in a warm oven if you have any left over.

SERVES 6

Shortcrust pastry

500g plain white flour, plus extra to dust

generous pinch of sea salt

250g unsalted butter, well chilled, cut into little cubes

1 organic free-range large egg yolk

2–3 tbsp cool water

1 organic free-range egg, lightly beaten, to glaze

Filling

1 organic free-range chicken, about 1.5kg

2 celery sticks, roughly chopped

6 carrots, peeled and chopped

10 black peppercorns

3 bay leaves

small bunch of thyme

small bunch of parsley

2 tbsp unsalted butter

2 tbsp plain flour

150ml crème fraîche

sea salt and freshly ground black pepper

bunch of flat-leaf parsley, stalks removed, roughly chopped

To make the pastry, sift the flour and salt into a bowl and rub in the butter lightly and evenly until the mixture resembles breadcrumbs. Lightly beat the egg yolk with the water, then sprinkle over the flour. Work gently with your fingertips to form a dough, adding a little more water if necessary. Form into a ball and knead lightly on a floured surface. Wrap in baking parchment and rest in the fridge for 1 hour, or until needed.

For the filling, wash and pat dry the chicken, removing any giblets and/ or fat deposits from inside the cavity. Place the chicken in a cooking pot, large enough to hold it comfortably and add the celery, a third of the carrots, the peppercorns and herbs. Pour on enough water to cover the chicken and place over a medium heat. Bring to the boil, then immediately lower the heat to a gentle simmer and poach for 1 hour. Remove from the heat and leave the chicken to cool in its liquor.

Simmer the rest of the carrots in a pan of salted water until just tender, about 7–10 minutes; drain and set aside.

Once the chicken is completely cooled, lift it out onto a board. Strain the liquor and reserve 500ml for the pie (keep the rest to use as stock). Tear the chicken into generous pieces, discarding the skin. Set aside.

Melt the butter in a saucepan, stir in the flour and cook, stirring, over a very low heat for a minute or so, without colouring. Slowly stir in the reserved liquor and cook, stirring, for 5 minutes, or until the sauce has thickened. Add the crème fraîche, season generously and take off the heat. If the sauce is at all lumpy, pass through a sieve. Stir through the chopped parsley and leave to cool.

Divide the pastry in two, making one portion slightly bigger than the other. Re-wrap the smaller one (for the lid) and return to the fridge.

Roll out the other portion on a floured surface to a round, large enough to line a 20cm fluted pie tin, about 3cm deep; the round will need to be at least 28cm in diameter. Lift the pastry into the tin, press it evenly onto the base and sides, then trim the edge. Prick the base lightly with a fork. Chill for 15 minutes. Meanwhile, preheat the oven to 180°C/Gas 4.

Line the pastry case with a piece of baking parchment and half-fill with baking beans (or dried beans). Bake the pastry case on the middle shelf of the oven for 15 minutes, then remove the paper and beans and bake for a further 5 minutes to slightly dry out the base. Set aside to cool a little.

In the meantime, roll out the other piece of pastry thinly to a round, 5mm thick, for the pie lid.

Spoon the chicken mixture into the pastry case, then using a rolling pin, lift the pastry round over the top to cover. Press the pastry edges together with your fingertips to seal and mark a cross in the centre of the pie. Brush the pie generously with beaten egg and bake for 30 minutes until the pastry is golden brown and the filling is bubbling.

Leave the pie to stand on a wire rack for 5 minutes before serving, with buttered spinach.

❋ To line a flan tin, drape the pastry round over the tin and ease it in, leaving the excess pastry overhanging the rim of the tin. If using a fluted tin, press the pastry firmly into the flutes, being careful not to stretch it – I find this easiest to do using my thumbs. Then, using a sharp knife, cut away the excess pastry so that the pastry is level with the rim of the tin. Always prick the pastry base gently with a fork after lining the tin – this helps to prevent air bubbles from forming.

Buttered spinach

You may need to cook the spinach in a couple of batches, depending on the size of your saucepan. (Illustrated on previous page.)

SERVES 6

400g young spinach

40g unsalted butter

sea salt and freshly ground black pepper

½ tsp freshly grated nutmeg, or to taste

Wash the spinach in several changes of cold water to remove all traces of dirt. Put the spinach into a medium saucepan with just the water clinging to the leaves after washing. Allow to wilt over a low heat, stirring from time to time. Once all the spinach has wilted, drain in a colander, pressing firmly with the back of a wooden spoon to remove excess water.

Melt the butter in the pan, add the spinach and toss until it is really well coated. Season with salt, pepper and nutmeg to taste, then serve.

Caramelised blood oranges

I adore blood oranges. They usually first appear in December and stay around until March, but they're at their best during January and February. When you're unable to get hold of them, use another large, juicy variety of orange, such as Navel or Tarocco. This dessert can be assembled in minutes.

SERVES 6

6 blood oranges

Caramel

125g caster sugar

200ml water

First make the caramel. Put the sugar and 75ml water into a small heavy-based pan and place over a low heat. Stir once and then continue to warm, without stirring, until the sugar has completely dissolved. Now turn up the heat to fairly high and cook until a deep golden caramel has formed; this may take as long as 10 minutes. When it starts to colour, watch carefully, as it will darken quite quickly.

As soon as the caramel is a rich golden colour, carefully pour in the remaining 125ml water, protecting your hand with an oven glove or cloth because the mixture will hiss and spit. Cook, stirring, for another couple of minutes or so until the caramel thins and is smooth. Pour into a heatproof bowl and allow to cool, then chill in the fridge.

To prepare the oranges, using a small sharp knife, slice off the base and top of the oranges, then stand upright on a board. Working the knife from top to bottom, cut away the peel and pith in sections following the contour of the fruit. Now slice the oranges across into pinwheels, about 3mm thick.

Arrange the orange slices in a shallow serving dish and pour the chilled caramel over them to serve.

Retro dinner

Veal and pork meatloaf
Tomato and herb sauce
Braised artichokes
Leafy salad dressed with hazelnut
vinaigrette

*

Fresh fruit or fruit compote
(see page 17)

Veal and pork meatloaf

Meatloaf may sound unappealing, but this one is truly delicious – I find the combination of veal and pork works particularly well. The trick lies in the seasoning – it should be lively, vibrant and warm. A succulent texture is also important; there is nothing more unpalatable than a dry meatloaf. You can prepare it in advance and keep it in the fridge, ready to bake and serve. (Illustrated on previous page.)

SERVES 6

olive oil, for oiling

500g organic pork, minced

500g organic veal, minced

100g fresh white breadcrumbs

3 garlic cloves, peeled and crushed

150g Parmesan cheese, freshly grated

handful of marjoram or sage leaves, finely chopped

1 dried red chilli

sea salt and freshly ground black pepper

Preheat the oven to 200°C/Gas 6. Lightly oil a 23 x 13cm (900g) loaf tin.

Put the minced meat into a large bowl and add the breadcrumbs, garlic, Parmesan and marjoram or sage. Crumble in the dried chilli and season generously, especially with salt – it brings this dish to life. Mix together really well, using your hands, until the ingredients are well combined.

To check the seasoning, take a little of the meat mixture and form into a small patty. Fry in a lightly oiled pan for a couple of minutes on each side. Let cool slightly and then taste. This way you get a clear idea of the seasoning – you can then adjust the seasoning of the mixture accordingly.

Spoon the meat mixture into the loaf tin, pressing it down firmly with your hands. Cook on the middle shelf of the oven for 30 minutes, then lower the oven setting to 180°C/Gas 4 and bake for a further 15 minutes.

Leave to stand for a few minutes before turning out onto a warm serving platter. Cut the meat loaf into 2–3cm thick slices and serve with the tomato and herb sauce spooned over.

Tomato and herb sauce

Herby, slightly sharp, mellow and punchy all at the same time, this sauce adds a certain something to the meatloaf that I feel completes the dish. (Illustrated on previous page.)

SERVES 6

12 little ripe plum tomatoes

1 garlic clove, peeled and crushed

3 rosemary sprigs, leaves only, finely chopped

sea salt and freshly ground black pepper

1 tbsp Dijon mustard

1½ tsp red wine vinegar

2 tbsp extra virgin olive oil

small bunch of flat-leaf parsley, chopped

75g fresh white breadcrumbs

handful of black olives

Preheat the oven to 200°C/Gas 6. Pierce each tomato with a sharp knife – this helps them release their juice during cooking. Place the tomatoes on a baking tray and roast in the oven for 15 minutes. Set aside to cool.

Meanwhile, using a pestle and mortar, pound the garlic and rosemary with a good pinch of salt to a paste. Add the mustard and wine vinegar and stir to combine. Add the tomatoes and crush roughly.

Add the olive oil, chopped parsley and breadcrumbs and stir well to combine. Stir in the olives and season with salt and pepper to taste.

Leafy salad dressed with hazelnut vinaigrette

A simply dressed, clean-tasting leafy salad is a lovely palate-cleansing accompaniment to this menu, as it balances out the more robust food. A variety of leaves works well here – some bitter, some soft and sweet, with a few herb leaves thrown in too for good measure.

SERVES 6

6 large handfuls of assorted salad leaves, such as sorrel, frisée, rocket, purslane, baby spinach and/or chard

handful of herb leaves, such as fennel, chervil and/or parsley

Dressing

1½ tsp Dijon mustard

1 tbsp sherry vinegar

sea salt and freshly ground black pepper

3 tbsp extra virgin olive oil

2 tbsp hazelnut oil

squeeze of lemon juice, to taste

Rinse the salad and herb leaves in a bowl of cool water, then drain and pat dry – very gently. Place in a bowl, tearing larger leaves such as frisée into smaller pieces.

For the dressing, whisk the mustard and sherry vinegar together in a bowl with a pinch each of salt and pepper. Whisk in the olive oil followed by the hazelnut oil to emulsify, then add a squeeze of lemon juice to taste.

Drizzle the dressing over the salad and toss lightly, using your fingertips. Pile onto a serving plate.

Braised artichokes

Artichokes start to appear in shops and markets around the end of February. I prefer to use the smaller ones with tightly closed buds and very often purple-tipped leaves; the heart inside is usually tender with hardly any choke. Select artichokes that feel heavy for their size, without any discolouration or bruising. If you are preparing the artichokes ahead, immerse them in a bowl of cool water with a little lemon juice added – this will prevent them from discolouring.

SERVES 6

6 artichokes, stalks intact

salt and freshly ground black pepper

2 tbsp virgin olive oil

2 garlic cloves, peeled and finely chopped

small handful of mint, leaves only, finely chopped

small handful of flat-leaf parsley, leaves only, finely chopped

1 bay leaf

250ml verjus or dry white wine

To prepare the artichokes (illustrated overleaf), tear off the tough outer leaves by pulling them down to the stem. Keep going until you come to the soft leaves in the centre that are attached to the heart. Now, using a small sharp knife, trim the heart and slice off the end of the stalk 2–3cm below the base of the heart. Trim off the pointy tips of the leaves. Slice the artichokes in half lengthways and scoop out any hairy choke, using a teaspoon. Season the artichoke halves with salt and pepper.

Place a heavy-based pan over a low heat and add 1 tbsp olive oil. Place the artichoke halves in the pan – they should fit quite tightly. Sprinkle with the garlic, mint and parsley, and add the bay leaf. Turn the heat up slightly. Once the pan is sizzling, pour in the verjus or wine.

Place a lid on the pan, turn the heat right down and cook gently for 25–30 minutes until the artichokes are tender and the liquid is more or less evaporated. Remove the lid, turn up the heat once more and drizzle over the remaining 1 tbsp olive oil. Cook over high heat for a minute or so, to allow the artichokes to brown a little. Serve at once.

Verjus (or verjuice) is a slightly sour juice made from unripe grapes. Available from selected supermarkets and specialist food suppliers, it lends a special flavour, but dry white wine can be substituted.

Late night supper

When you are eating later in the evening – perhaps after the theatre or cinema – it is important to have something simple and light. Of course, it often seems easier just to grab something in a restaurant on the way back, but a late evening supper at home is quieter, less frenetic and more engaging. Planning is key and as far as possible the preparation needs to be done in advance. So, when you return, there is little to do other than to finish off and warm through whatever you are serving, dress a salad and – if the mood takes you – lay out one perfectly ripe cheese and a little fruit or dessert.

The most elegant food of all is often the simplest – where less is more. Keep the table low key, too. Supper in the kitchen is comforting and casual and lends itself perfectly to this kind of eating. The memory of a wonderful meal does not simply comprise the food that was eaten, but also the friends it was spent with, the place it was eaten in... simplicity allows you to remember it all just that much more vividly.

Prepare ahead

Clam and corn chowder
Pulled bread
Tomato salad
*
Ripe figs

Clam and corn chowder

Sweet late summer corn and clams – with their salty flavour of the sea – are a delicious combination. Add just a hint of chilli and you have a dish that is beautifully rounded, heartwarming and perfect to eat later in the evening, perhaps after the theatre or cinema, or a long day at work. Prepare the chowder base earlier in the day, adding the clams just before serving.

SERVES 6

100g unsalted butter

1 large yellow onion, peeled and finely chopped

1 large carrot, peeled and chopped

2 celery sticks, chopped

1 fennel bulb, tough outer layer removed, chopped

1 small red chilli, deseeded and very finely chopped

2 bay leaves

1 garlic clove, peeled and finely chopped

sea salt and freshly ground black pepper

3 corn-on-the-cobs

700ml water

1kg fresh clams

150ml double cream (optional, but a good addition)

Melt the butter in a large heavy-based saucepan over a medium-low heat. Add the onion, carrot, celery, fennel, chilli, bay leaves and garlic. Stir until all the vegetables are well coated in butter, then reduce the heat to low and cook until tender, about 15 minutes. Season with a good pinch of salt.

In the meantime, cut the corn from the cobs. The easiest way to do this is to stand the cob upright on a board and run a sharp knife down in sections. Discard any stringy bits and try to save the milky juices.

Add the corn and juices to the softened vegetables and pour in the water. Stir well and increase the heat to medium. Bring to a simmer and cook until the corn is tender but still retains a little bite, about 20 minutes.

Pour the soup into a sieve set over a bowl to save the liquor. Discard the bay leaves. Tip half of the vegetables into a blender or food processor and add half of the cooking liquid. Process to a very smooth purée – it will be quite thick. Pass through a fine sieve into a large, clean saucepan, pressing on the vegetables to extract as much liquid as possible.

Add the rest of the vegetables to the pan, place over a low heat and stir well to combine. Stir in as much of the remaining liquor as required to give the desired consistency. (You can prepare the chowder ahead to this point and set aside until ready to eat.)

Pick over the clams, discarding any that are damaged or open and do not close when gently squeezed. To clean, wash under cold running water to remove superficial grit, then immerse in a bowl of cold water and leave to soak in the fridge for 20 minutes.

When ready to serve, bring the soup to a simmer over a medium-high heat. Drain the clams and add them to the pan. Cover the pan with a tight-fitting lid and cook for about 3 minutes until the clams open, stirring once or twice to encourage them to do so and immediately re-covering.

Once all the clams are open (discard any that refuse to do so), stir in the cream if using. Taste and adjust the seasoning, adding plenty of pepper and possibly a little salt if needed.

Ladle into a warm soup tureen, place on the table and serve, along with the warm bread.

When laying down the foundation of a dish – such as onions, garlic, herbs and chilli – cook slowly over the lowest possible heat. The base flavours will develop sweetness and mellow with gentle cooking – ready to enhance rather than overpower the main ingredients of your dish. So don't rush, be patient...

Pulled bread

The beauty of this bread is that it is quick and foolproof to make. There is no yeast involved, so you don't need to allow time for rising. It has a lovely thick chewy crust and a fairly dense texture and is best served warm. If the fancy takes you, dip the bread into the soup – it will soak up all the wonderful flavours without falling apart. (Also illustrated on page 176.)

SERVES 6

450g plain white flour, plus extra to dust

1 tsp salt

1 tsp bicarbonate of soda

375ml milk

Preheat the oven to 220°C/Gas 7. Sift the dry ingredients into a large bowl. Make a well in the centre and pour in most of the milk all at once. Using one hand, stir in a circular fashion, gradually mixing in the flour from the sides of the bowl, adding a little more milk as necessary. The dough should be soft, but not wet and sticky.

Once the dough has come together, turn it out onto a well-floured surface and knead very lightly for a few seconds only. Now shape it into a long thin sausage, bend in the middle to form a U-shape and plait loosely.

Place on a baking sheet and bake in the oven for 15 minutes, then lower the oven setting to 200°C/Gas 6 and bake for a further 15 minutes, or until cooked. To test, tap the bread on the bottom with your knuckles – it should sound hollow. Transfer to a wire rack to cool, but serve still slightly warm, with lightly salted butter.

Make the bread earlier in the day if you like. Before serving, simply warm the loaf in the oven, preheated to 200°C/Gas 6 for 5 minutes or so.

Tomato salad

A tomato salad is the perfect match for the corn chowder. Tomatoes are at their best during the late summer months when fresh corn is also ready to be picked. Perfectly ripe and sweet, I like to enjoy them just as they are, with no more than a drizzle of verdantly green extra olive oil and a sprinkling of coarse sea salt and herbs.

SERVES 6

6 large, ripe tomatoes (unblemished)

coarse sea salt and freshly ground black pepper

small handful of soft-leafed thyme or basil leaves

100g young, light goat's cheese, such as fleur de chèvre (optional)

good-quality extra virgin olive oil, to drizzle

Slice the tomatoes into wedges and pile onto a serving plate. Season with a little salt and pepper, and scatter over some fragrant thyme or torn basil leaves – ideally straight from the garden.

Crumble the goat's cheese over the salad if using. Finally drizzle with extra virgin olive oil.

Quick and easy

Oeufs en cocotte with spinach and Parma ham
*
Blackberry crisp

Oeufs en cocotte with spinach and Parma ham

I think of this comforting little egg dish as something to be eaten in the evening rather than for breakfast. Its light nature makes it perfect for a late-night supper and its simplicity is very appealing. As long as the spinach has been prepared beforehand there is very little to do, except heat the oven and crack the eggs. (Also illustrated on previous page.)

SERVES 4

200g small young
spinach leaves

sea salt and freshly
ground black pepper

knob of unsalted butter

8 slices of Parma, San
Daniele or Bayonne
ham, roughly torn

4 organic free-range
large eggs

4 tbsp double cream

freshly grated nutmeg,
to taste

50g Parmesan cheese,
freshly grated

rustic bread, to serve

Prepare the spinach in advance (in the afternoon, perhaps). Wash the leaves thoroughly to remove all traces of dirt and drain well. Place a large, dry pan over a low heat and add the spinach. Cook briefly until the spinach has just wilted – no additional water is needed as the water clinging to the leaves after washing is enough. Drain and set aside until the spinach is cold enough to handle.

In batches, squeeze the spinach with your hands to get rid of excess water and place in a bowl. Season with salt and pepper, then cover and refrigerate until needed.

When you are ready to eat, preheat the oven to 200°C/Gas 6. Place the blanched spinach in a pan with a knob of butter to warm through. Season with a little more pepper to taste. Divide equally among 4 ramekins (about 200ml capacity). Arrange the Parma ham on top.

Crack an egg into each ramekin and spoon over the cream. Finish with a sprinkling of nutmeg and Parmesan, and a generous grinding of pepper.

Stand the ramekins in a roasting tin and pour in enough hot water to come two-thirds of the way up the side of the dishes. Cook on the middle shelf of the oven for about 8 minutes; the white should be set, with the yolk still soft.

Carefully lift the ramekins out of the bain-marie. Serve on small plates, with a folded napkin underneath the ramekins to secure them, and rustic bread alongside.

Very fresh, free-range

organic eggs will make all the difference to this dish. As you crack open each one, the white should be viscous and buoyant, and the yolk glossy and a warm yellow colour.

Blackberry crisp

This is possibly the simplest dessert to make. However, don't be tempted to substitute another fruit – it's not the same without the bursting flavour of ripe blackberries – even raspberries won't do here as their water content is too high. A caramely crumble with a hint of orange is the ideal topping.

SERVES 4

350g blackberries

2 tbsp caster sugar

finely grated zest of
1 large orange

Topping

75g plain white flour

50g dark muscovado
sugar

finely grated zest of
1 large orange

75g chilled unsalted
butter, cut into cubes

Preheat the oven to 200°C/Gas 6. Place the blackberries in a bowl and scatter over the caster sugar and orange zest. Toss together lightly, using your fingers, then spoon into an ovenproof serving dish.

For the topping, combine the flour and brown sugar in another bowl and stir in the orange zest. Now rub in the cubes of chilled butter, using your fingertips, until the mixture is the texture of wet sand – don't overwork – little lumps of butter and sugar give a better result.

Scatter the topping over the blackberries and place the dish on the middle shelf of the oven. Bake for 15–20 minutes, or until the topping is golden brown and the blackberries burst and ooze their inky black juice.

Allow to cool slightly for a few minutes before serving, with a jug of chilled cream alongside.

Wild blackberries or 'brambles' can be found almost everywhere along hedgerows during the summer and early autumn. Pick the softest, heaviest fruit that has fully ripened in the sun.

Italian influence

Bagna cauda

*

Gnudi with sage butter

*

Roasted persimmons

My all-time, ultimate late-night supper. To eat it makes me feel that I am somewhere isolated, perhaps at the top of a snow-covered mountain, wrapped up warm with a log fire burning and in the company of good friends.

Bagna cauda

This is a lovely Italian sharing dish from the northern region of Piedmont. Bagna cauda – literally hot bath – is a piquant anchovy-based sauce in which vegetables are dipped (or bathed) and eaten with the fingers. Jerusalem artichokes and cardoons (which the Italians call gobi*) are authentic accompaniments.*

Typically, the sauce is kept warm on a little tabletop stove. Often, when all the vegetables and sauce have been eaten, an egg is cracked into the pan and stirred until silky and scrambled.

SERVES 4–6

200ml mild-tasting extra virgin olive oil

150g unsalted butter

12 good-quality tinned anchovies or from a jar (Ortiz, for example), chopped

1 garlic clove, peeled and crushed

finely grated zest of 1 lemon

freshly ground black pepper

To serve

selection of vegetables for dipping, such as cardoons, Jerusalem artichokes, small new potatoes, little carrots, fennel, celery and radishes

rustic bread

Put the olive oil, butter, anchovies, garlic and lemon zest into a pan over a very low heat and add a few grindings of pepper. Stir constantly until the butter melts and the anchovies disintegrate – you should have a thick, homogenised, sludgy pale brown sauce. Taste and adjust the seasoning if necessary.

To prepare the vegetables: peel the cardoons and boil for 15–20 minutes; scrub the Jerusalem artichokes clean and boil for 15–20 minutes; scrub the new potatoes and boil for about 15 minutes until just tender. Drain the boiled vegetables thoroughly. Carrots, fennel, celery and radishes are served raw: simply clean and slice the fennel and celery. Arrange the vegetables on a serving platter.

Serve the bagna cauda with the dipping vegetables and crusty, open-pored bread, which can be similarly dragged through the sauce.

Gnudi with sage butter

Gnudi – literally naked – are soft delicate dumplings flavoured simply with ricotta, Parmesan and nutmeg – ingredients that are typically combined for a ravioli filling. Effectively it is a dish of 'naked ravioli', without the pasta covering, hence the name. Use either sheep's or buffalo milk ricotta if possible – both are lovely and delicate – otherwise fresh cow's milk ricotta will still give good results. (Illustrated on previous page and page 188.)

SERVES 4–6

500g fresh ricotta

1 tsp freshly grated nutmeg

120g Parmesan cheese, freshly grated, plus extra to serve

sea salt and freshly ground black pepper

500g semolina flour

150g unsalted butter

handful of sage leaves

Put the ricotta in a sieve and set aside for about 20 minutes to allow any excess liquid to drain away; this stage is important – don't skip it.

Now place the drained ricotta in a bowl and beat well with a fork until light and fluffy. Stir in the grated nutmeg and Parmesan until well combined, then season the mixture generously with salt and pepper. Cover and place in the fridge for an hour to chill.

Scatter half of the semolina over a flat baking tray; it should cover the tray evenly. Scatter the rest evenly onto a clean surface and flour your hands.

Take a third of the chilled ricotta mixture in your hands and roll into a sausage shape, about 3cm in diameter (illustrated on previous page). Place on the floured surface and slice into 3cm lengths. Using floured hands, roll each piece into a little roughly shaped ball, coat in the flour on the work surface and then place on the baking tray.

Continue in this way until all the mixture is shaped into dumplings and set on the tray. Give the tray a shake to ensure that all the gnudi are well coated with flour and place in the fridge overnight.

When ready to cook, place a large, wide pan of well-salted water on to boil. You will need to cook the gnudi in batches to avoid overcrowding the pan. Once the water is boiling vigorously, drop in a third of the dumplings and cook for 3 minutes, or until they rise to the surface indicating that they are ready. Remove the gnudi carefully with a slotted spoon (they are very fragile) and let drain in the spoon for a few moments.

While the gnudi are cooking, gently melt the butter in a large, wide pan over a low heat along with the sage leaves. Using a slotted spoon, carefully place the gnudi in the pan. Spoon the sage-infused butter over the gnudi to ensure they are well coated.

Divide the gnudi among warm serving bowls, spoon over the sage butter and scatter over a little Parmesan.

Roasted persimmons

Like all fruit, persimmons need to be eaten when they are properly ripe. They are around in late autumn, though sadly, in this country the fruit is often sold when small and hard – tasting not much of anything. In Italy, where persimmons are much loved, they are eaten so ripe that their skin is almost bursting and the flesh is soft and sweet with a wonderful, decadent flavour. Fully ripe fruit is very fragile and should be handled gently – it can be eaten simply peeled, just as it is. Here I have opted to roast the fruit lightly with vanilla and honey.

SERVES 4–6

6 ripe persimmons

3 tbsp clean light flavoured honey

1 vanilla pod, split lengthways

Preheat the oven to 200°C/Gas 6. Using your fingers, peel the skin from the fruit – it should come away easily. Cut the persimmons in half and place on a baking tray (preferably non-stick). Drizzle with the honey and poke the split vanilla pod in between the fruit. Roast in the oven for 10 minutes. Serve warm, with pouring cream.

Special occasion

There is no better way to mark a celebration than with food. The taste, smell and sight of beautiful food in an agreeable setting create more happy memories than any other single thing I can think of. As a child, these occasions always felt like a thrilling treat to me. I remember great quantities of things made with love, care and attention – freshly churned ice cream, home-made bread and platters piled high with my favourite things. Food was chosen and prepared with consideration of everyone's favourite things to eat.

Special occasions are about spending time with those you love, not cooking in the kitchen, so I like to prepare as much of the food as possible in advance. The following menus are composed with this in mind and for the most part the dishes can be created well ahead. Think about the setting, too. Laying an elegant table will only enhance your special meal.

The one really magical thing about these memorable occasions is that you can almost be certain that the table will be shared with those closest to you.

Christmas Eve

Oysters with mignonette sauce
Baked ham
Braised red cabbage
Dauphinoise potatoes
*
Pashka
Vacherin with walnuts and
Muscat grapes

Oysters with mignonette sauce

I didn't really begin to enjoy oysters until my mid-twenties. When I was younger they looked strange and unappealing to me. And I didn't like being coerced into eating them. 'I dare you,' or 'Please, just have a go,' only served to make me more suspicious. These days, however, my eyes light up with excitement even at the prospect of eating one. As they suggest luxury, they're perfect to eat on Christmas Eve.

I like to eat oysters more or less unadorned – with a squeeze of lemon juice, a drop or two of Tabasco or this simple shallot and sherry vinegar dressing – or with nothing at all. You can open them an hour or so prior to eating and leave them sitting on their half-shell nestling in their natural juices, ready to serve. (Illustrated on previous page.)

SERVES 8

5 fresh live oysters
per person

Mignonette sauce

250ml good-quality
sherry vinegar

4 large shallots, or
6 smaller ones, peeled
and diced

pinch of sea salt

To serve

coarse sea salt

For the dressing, pour the sherry vinegar into a bowl, stir in the diced shallots and season with a pinch of salt.

Shuck the oysters, being careful to retain their juices, and arrange them in their half-shell on a bed of sea salt on individual plates.

Serve with the sherry vinegar and shallot dressing on the side for guests to spoon onto their oysters.

To shuck an oyster,

hold firmly in a folded tea towel with the flatter shell uppermost and insert an oyster knife into the hinge of the shell. Keeping the oyster level, so you don't lose too much of the precious juice, twist the knife a bit to open up the shell and sever the hinge muscle. Lift off the top shell. Slide the knife under the oyster in the bottom half-shell to release it and remove any fragments of shell from the oyster.

Baked ham

My mother always cooks a wonderful ham at Christmas, serving it with a fresh mango chutney, sharpened with lime juice and finished with coriander. She also accompanies it with a salad, consisting of roasted beetroot, creamy mellow feta and walnuts, which we all love. It's funny how food ritual makes for the best memories. Here I'm serving the ham with more traditional accompaniments. A pot of good mustard is a welcome addition, but spiced fruits add another dimension altogether. (Illustrated overleaf.)

A large ham will provide plenty for everyone and leave you with a sizeable joint to carve and serve at room temperature with salads, or with eggs for breakfast, or in sandwiches in the days after Christmas.

SERVES 8, PLUS EXTRA
TO SERVE LATER

5–6kg ham (naturally salted), ideally on the bone

3 celery sticks, roughly chopped

1 yellow onion, peeled and cut into wedges

4 carrots, peeled and roughly chopped

12 black peppercorns

4 bay leaves

Glaze

2 tbsp Dijon mustard

3 tbsp soft brown sugar

finely grated zest and juice of 1 orange

handful of cloves

150ml white wine

To serve

Dijon or other mustard

Spiced pears (see page 236)

Put the ham to soak in a large bowl of cold water for at least 12 hours before cooking to remove excess salt.

Put the vegetables into a large stockpot or heavy-based pan that is large enough to hold the ham comfortably. Place the ham on top of them and pour over enough water to cover the ham completely. Add the peppercorns and bay leaves.

Cover the pan with a tight-fitting lid and set over a medium heat. Once the water has come to the boil, turn down the heat. Allow the ham to simmer gently for 3–3½ hours, depending on size, topping up the water as necessary – it is important that the ham is completely submerged throughout the simmering process. When the ham is cooked, the meat will be firm and opaque. Remove from the heat and leave the ham to cool in its liquor to room temperature.

Preheat the oven to 180°C/Gas 4. Lift the ham out of the pan and place on a board. Discard the liquor.

For the glaze, mix the mustard, brown sugar and orange zest and juice together in a bowl.

Remove the skin from the ham, leaving most of the fat layer in place. Score the fat in a diamond pattern and stud each diamond with a clove. Spoon the glaze evenly over the top. Place the ham in a roasting tin and pour the wine around the ham. Roast for about 20–30 minutes until the glaze is a glistening rich colour and slightly set. Set aside until you are ready to serve. Accompany with a pot of mustard and Spiced pears.

One of the most invaluable

things to have is a set of good-quality sharp knives that are well looked after. They make life so much easier in the kitchen. Sharp knifes are safer to use than blunt ones and they make chopping and slicing quicker and less arduous. Buy a steel and use to sharpen your knives regularly; wash and dry knives by hand after use and store them separately in a knife rack or drawer.

Braised red cabbage

This beguiling sweet-sour vegetable dish has a festive, wintry feel and is perfect served alongside the glazed ham. It is the colour and shine of a Christmas bauble catching the light of a candle.

SERVES 8

50g unsalted butter

1 medium red onion, peeled and finely sliced

1 tsp cloves

4–5 juniper berries

3 bay leaves

2 Bramleys or other sharp cooking apples

2 tbsp raisins

1 medium red cabbage

2 tbsp good-quality red wine vinegar

3 tbsp caster sugar

sea salt and freshly ground black pepper

2 tbsp aged balsamic vinegar

Melt the butter in a large heavy-based pan over a low heat, then add the onion, cloves, juniper berries and bay leaves and cook over a low heat for 15 minutes, or until the onion is very soft and translucent, stirring from time to time. Meanwhile, quarter and core the apples, but don't bother to remove the skin.

Add the apples and raisins to the pan and cook for a further 10 minutes. Meanwhile, discard the outer leaves from the cabbage, then slice into quarters and cut out the core. Shred the cabbage fairly finely.

Add the wine vinegar and sugar to the pan and stir until the sugar has dissolved, then add the cabbage. Cover and cook for 30 minutes until the cabbage is very tender, stirring every now and then to ensure that it does not stick to the base of the pan. Season with salt and plenty of pepper.

Turn off the heat and leave to stand for an hour or so, to allow the flavours to get to know one another. Before serving, add the balsamic vinegar and reheat gently. Taste the seasoning and adjust as necessary.

Serve the braised cabbage steaming hot – the aroma of cloves and juniper will fill the room.

Dauphinoise potatoes

These rich, soft creamy potatoes, tasting of nutmeg and garlic, are heavenly served with thick slices of glazed ham. It is important to use Gruyère here; its delicate flavour and relatively low fat content (for a hard cheese) lend a more refined taste than, say, Cheddar. And do use waxy rather than floury potatoes; traditionally these are cut as finely as possible, but I like them with a little more body.

SERVES 8

1.5–1.7kg Desirée potatoes, peeled

1 litre whole milk

sea salt and freshly ground pepper

600ml double cream or crème fraîche

3 garlic cloves, peeled and very finely sliced

1–1½ tsp freshly grated nutmeg, to taste

250g Gruyère, grated

Cut the potatoes into 3mm thick slices. Place in a large saucepan, pour over the milk and add a good pinch of salt. If the potatoes are not completely submerged, top up with a little water. Bring to a gentle simmer over a medium heat and cook until the potatoes are just tender when pierced with a fork; this will take about 15 minutes. Drain in a colander, discarding the milk.

Preheat the oven to 200°C/Gas 6. Tip the warm potatoes into a large bowl and pour over the cream or crème fraîche. Season generously with salt and pepper and add the garlic and nutmeg. Toss to ensure the potatoes are well coated, then taste for seasoning and add a little more salt and pepper if needed.

Transfer to an ovenproof serving dish, spreading the potatoes out evenly. Scatter over the grated cheese, ensuring that it is evenly distributed, and place in the oven. Bake for 20–25 minutes until golden brown on top and the cream is bubbling seductively underneath.

Freshly grated nutmeg has a lovely sweet, spicy fragrance. It is far superior to the ready-ground nutmeg sold in jars, which can taste musty... so please always grate your own.

Pashka

Originating in Russia, this romantic, beautiful and unusual dessert has a sense of occasion. Studded with candied peel, raisins and almonds, the sweet curd cheese mixture is rich without question, but not heavy. To me, it feels like Christmas, without taking away from the more traditional plum pudding that is to follow the next day. Making pashka is a fairly lengthy process, but worth the effort, which always seems appropriate in the festive season. Here I've concealed the filling for a pure, clean appearance and to give guests a surprise. I have served it with very ripe persimmon, but pashka is also lovely just as it is.

SERVES 10–12

900g soft curd cheese

6 organic free-range large eggs

300g unsalted butter

225g caster sugar

250ml double cream

1 vanilla pod, halved lengthways

50g raisins

1 tbsp vodka

25g blanched almonds, chopped

50g good-quality candied peel

grated zest of 1 lemon

grated zest of 1 orange

To serve

1 ripe persimmon, cut into fine wedges, or candied fruit (see page 218)

Allow the curd cheese, eggs and butter to stand for an hour at room temperature; if the cheese is very moist, place it in a colander to drain.

Using an electric mixer, beat the curd cheese for 5 minutes until smooth. Break the eggs into a separate bowl and beat, using a hand-held whisk, until thick and pale gold, then add the sugar and beat once again until well combined. Pour the cream into a saucepan and just bring to a simmer, then remove from the heat and set aside.

With the electric mixer on its lowest setting, beat the egg mixture into the curd cheese, then slowly incorporate the warm cream, keeping the mixture smooth. Transfer the mixture to a heatproof bowl and place over a pan of simmering water, making sure the bowl is not in direct contact with the water. Add the vanilla pod and cook, stirring constantly with a wooden spoon, for about 30 minutes until the mixture thickens substantially.

Meanwhile, soak the raisins in the vodka for 15 minutes or so.

Strain the curd cheese mixture in batches through a sieve into a clean bowl, rubbing it through with a firm spatula. Transfer one third to a separate bowl. Stir the raisins, almonds, candied peel and the citrus zests into the rest of the mixture. Cover both bowls and chill well for 1–2 hours.

Using an electric mixer, beat the butter until soft, then fold into the chilled curd mixture until evenly blended.

Line a 1.7–2 litre mould with muslin, allowing enough overhang to cover the top. Spoon in the plain curd cheese mixture to cover the bottom and sides, then spoon the rest into the middle. Fold the muslin over the top to enclose. Place in the fridge to chill for 12 hours before serving.

To unmould the pashka, draw back the muslin from the surface, place a serving dish over the top and invert. Peel off the muslin gently and leave to stand for an hour in a cool place before serving. Top with wedges of ripe persimmon – or slices of home-made candied fruit.

Depending on what we have planned for the following day, I might leave off the dessert from this menu and have a simple bowl of sweet clementines instead, though I adore pashka – it always makes me think of snow, warm fires and Christmas.

Vacherin with walnuts and Muscat grapes

One of the few truly seasonal cheeses, vacherin becomes available in early December, heralding the start of Christmas festivities. By February it will be gone for another year. Traditionally it is served very slightly warm, which brings out its sweet, nutty flavour and enhances its creamy texture.

Here I'm serving it with young, still slightly wet walnuts and Muscat grapes – both are perfect to nibble alongside. If possible, buy dried Muscat grapes, which have an intensely sweet raisin flavour.

Normally I would serve cheese before the dessert course as they do in France, but here I think it is better placed last – so guests can savour a morsel now and then as the evening moves forward. It's a way of celebrating the vacherin's brevity just a little longer.

SERVES 8

2 handfuls (or more) of fresh walnuts in their shells

1 vacherin, about 400g (see below)

2 tbsp walnut oil

bunch of
Muscat grapes

Preheat the oven to 160°C/Gas 2½. Meanwhile, gently crack open the walnuts – I use a wooden rolling pin rather than a nutcracker – leaving them in their half-shells.

Place the walnuts on a small baking tray. Remove the lid from the vacherin and place on another small baking tray. Place the baking trays side by side on the middle shelf of the oven and warm both through for about 10 minutes. The cheese should be soft and warm to the touch, but not oozing.

Spoon the walnut oil over the nuts. Place the cheese on a board and arrange the nuts and grapes alongside. Provide a large serving spoon, for vacherin should always be spooned rather than sliced.

Vacherin is produced both in Switzerland and France. The Swiss version, Vacherin Mont d'Or, is made from pasteurised milk, while the French version, Vacherin du Haut Doubs, uses unpasteurised milk. The cheese is available in several sizes, usually 400g, 800g and 1.2kg. Buy a medium-sized cheese if you are serving 10–12, allowing an extra 5 minutes in the oven. Also bear in mind that once it has been warmed, although still edible the following day, it won't be quite the same.

Easter Sunday

Carpaccio of wild sea bass

*

Slow-cooked lamb with
artichokes, peas and mint

*

Easter cake

Carpaccio of wild sea bass

A delicate and light starter is the perfect way to begin this celebratory meal. Clean, subtle and pure – with little more than olive oil and a squeeze of lemon – it's a gentle whisper to whet the appetite. Seasoning here is vital – too much will destroy all. Use a finely flaked sea salt, such as Maldon, scattering it lightly and evenly. The bass should be wild, firm in texture and absolutely fresh.

SERVES 6

750g filleted sea bass

6 tbsp mild-flavoured extra virgin olive oil (preferably Ligurian)

juice of 1 small lemon, or to taste

sea salt

Chill 6 large serving plates. The bass should also be well chilled. Take the fish out of the fridge and cut into wafer-thin slices just before serving.

As you cut the fish, lay the slices directly onto the chilled plates, covering the base completely.

Drizzle 1 tbsp extra virgin olive oil over each serving and squeeze over a little lemon juice. Finish with a very light sprinkling of salt. Serve at once.

✺ Using a thin, sharp flexible-bladed knife, slice the fish off the skin, following the grain, cutting the slices as finely as possible – they should be almost translucent.

Slow-cooked lamb with artichokes, peas and mint

In Rome, peas and artichokes are a typical combination, often with broad beans too. Here the vegetables are cooked slowly, together with the lamb, which allows them to absorb the flavours of the meat juices. Traditionally this dish is eaten in the spring, when these vegetables make their first appearance.

SERVES 6

1 medium leg of lamb, trimmed of most fat

sea salt and freshly ground black pepper

1 tbsp olive oil

2 yellow onions, peeled and finely sliced

4 garlic cloves, peeled and crushed

3 bay leaves

1 dried red chilli, crumbled

small bunch of sage

small bunch of flat-leaf parsley

70ml red wine vinegar

300ml dry white wine

300ml light chicken stock

12 small purple artichokes, trimmed of outer leaves, stems removed

200g freshly podded peas

Preheat the oven to 200°C/Gas 6. Season the meat all over with salt and pepper. Place a large heavy-based roasting tin over a medium heat and allow it to get really hot. Add the olive oil, then lay the lamb in the tin and brown the meat really well on all sides; this will take about 15 minutes – it is important that the lamb is a good colour.

Once the meat is well browned, remove it from the pan and carefully pour off any fat, retaining the meat juices. Turn the heat to low and add the sliced onions, garlic, bay leaves, crumbled dried chilli and herbs to the roasting tin. Sweat gently for 10 minutes, stirring from time to time.

Now turn the heat to high and deglaze the pan with the wine vinegar and wine, scraping the bottom of the pan with a wooden spoon to release any sediment. The liquid should bubble and reduce a little; continue to stir the softened vegetables as the liquid reduces.

Pour in the stock and return the lamb to the pan. Cover tightly with foil and cook on the middle shelf of the oven for 20 minutes. Lower the oven setting to 170°C/Gas 3 and cook for 2 hours, still covered with the foil.

Now remove the foil and add the artichokes and peas to the roasting tin. Return to the oven and cook for a further 30 minutes, or until the artichokes are tender. Taste and adjust the seasoning. The meat should be so tender that it falls away from the bone.

Easter cake

As a child I remember going to a little café by the large train station in Sydney where they served very good hot chocolate and lots of different Italian cakes and pastries. We were allowed to choose something to eat and this was my favourite – rice, eggs and sugar combined together to make a simple not too sweet, soft cake. It hails from Bologna and is traditionally eaten at Easter time.

SERVES 8

1–1.2 litres milk

small pinch of salt

finely pared zest of 1 lemon (in a strip)

250g caster sugar

100g Arborio rice

melted butter, for greasing

25g fresh white breadcrumbs

4 organic free-range large eggs

1 organic free-range large egg yolk

grated zest of 1 lemon

grated zest of 1 orange

125g blanched almonds, chopped

2 tbsp Grand Marnier

To finish

Candied orange slices (see below)

Pour 1 litre milk into a heavy-based medium pan, add the salt, lemon zest strip and sugar and place over a medium-low heat. As soon as the milk comes to the boil, add the rice and stir well to combine. Turn the heat to its lowest possible setting and cook for 1–1¼ hours, stirring occasionally, until the rice is very soft and falling apart; if necessary add a little extra milk towards the end of cooking to prevent the rice sticking. Transfer to a large bowl, discard the lemon zest and set aside to cool slightly.

Preheat the oven to 170°C/Gas 3. Line the base of a 23cm round cake tin with baking parchment. Lightly butter the parchment and sides of the tin with melted butter and sprinkle with the breadcrumbs, tilting the tin to coat evenly and tipping out any excess crumbs.

Whisk the whole eggs and egg yolk together in a bowl until pale and mousse-like, then fold into the rice, a little at a time. Add the lemon and orange zest with the chopped almonds and fold in until evenly combined.

Pour the mixture into the prepared cake tin and bake on the middle shelf of the oven for 40–50 minutes until golden and firm to a light touch.

Place the cake tin on a wire rack. While the cake is still warm, prick the surface all over with a fine skewer and sprinkle with the Grand Marnier. Leave to cool.

When cool, run a knife around the inside of the tin and invert the cake onto a plate. Decorate with candied orange slices. Best served within 24 hours of making.

Candied fruit is a winter treat in itself. I make my own – often a combination of clementines, blood oranges, lemons and *cedro* (or citron) peel. It's easy to do. Simply slice the fruit, or in the case of *cedro*, first discard the small central area of flesh. Place in a saucepan of cold water, bring to a simmer and cook for 10 minutes, then drain; repeat this process three times. Now immerse the fruit in a sugar syrup (made using 100g sugar for every 100ml water) and simmer gently for approximately 30 minutes until translucent. Leave the fruit or peel to cool slowly in the syrup, then drain and leave to dry on a rack or a sheet of baking parchment overnight. Wrapped in parchment and stored in an airtight container in the fridge, the candied fruit or peel will keep for up to 4 months.

Birthday celebration

Freshly cooked lobster

Roasted pepper and chilli sauce

Mayonnaise (see page 81)

Roasted tomatoes with
basil and lemon

Potatoes with parsley, tarragon
and olive oil

Cucumber salad

Soda bread

*

Citrus tart

Freshly cooked lobster

In the UK we have some of the finest lobsters in the world, as our cold seas make for sweet, plump and firm flesh. Our lobsters also tend to be smaller than those found in warmer waters, so one per person is perfect. Buy them on the day you intend to serve them – they should be very definitely still alive when you get them home. In addition to the roasted pepper and chilli sauce, I like to serve a little pot of home-made mayonnaise on the side. Thick and unctuous, it is delicious smeared onto the lobster meat.

SERVES 4–6

4–6 very fresh live lobsters, about 500g each

sea salt and freshly ground black pepper

50g unsalted butter

To serve

lemon wedges

Mayonnaise
(see page 81)

Roasted pepper and chilli sauce
(see page 224)

Keep the lobsters covered with a damp cloth in the fridge. An hour or so before cooking, place them in the freezer – the intense cold will put them into a deep sleep.

To cook the lobsters, put a large pot of well-salted water on to boil. When it comes to a vigorous boil, plunge the lobsters in and cook for 7 minutes, then remove with a pair of tongs. Do not cook them any longer – overcooked lobster meat is not at all good to eat. Set aside until cool enough to handle.

To prepare the lobsters, first twist off the claws and set aside. Lay the lobsters on their backs on a board. Using a very sharp knife, cut through the middle of the soft underbelly to slice the tail meat in half lengthways. Crack open the claws and extract the meat. This can be done an hour or so ahead; if so cover the lobster and refrigerate.

Shortly before serving, place a large frying pan over a medium-high heat. (You may need to do this in two batches.) Add the butter, season the lobsters and lay them flat side down in the pan. Cook for 1 minute only, then turn and cook the underside for a little less than a minute – just enough to warm the flesh and give the outside the lightest colour.

Serve the lobsters on individual plates or large platters, with lemon wedges, mayonnaise and the roasted pepper and chilli sauce.

☼ I find the easiest way to remove the meat from the lobster claws is to tap them sharply, but not heavily with a rolling pin to crack the shells open. Then it should be possible to remove the meat in one piece.

Roasted tomatoes with basil and lemon

Roasted plum tomatoes pair beautifully with lobster, each enhancing the other's gentle sweetness.

SERVES 4–6

500g ripe plum tomatoes

80ml mild-tasting extra virgin olive oil

finely pared zest of 1–2 lemons

1 tsp caster sugar

sea salt and freshly ground black pepper

large handful of basil leaves

Preheat the oven to 180°C/Gas 4. Slice the tomatoes lengthways into quarters, place in a bowl and pour over the olive oil. Cut the lemon zest into shorter lengths and add to the tomatoes.

Add the sugar, a good pinch of salt and a few grindings of pepper. Tear over half of the basil leaves, toss all the ingredients together well and then transfer to a roasting tin.

Bake on the middle shelf of the oven for 20–25 minutes, or until the tomatoes are soft and very slightly blistered.

Tear over the remaining basil leaves and set aside to cool.

Roasted pepper and chilli sauce

I can't claim this sauce as my own. It was invented by my friend Kenny who worked with me in the kitchen at Petersham for a couple of years, before moving to Texas to open his own restaurant there. The sauce is mellow and sweet and works beautifully with the sweetness of the lobster.

SERVES 4–6

2 red peppers

1 red chilli

sea salt

200ml mild-tasting extra virgin olive oil

Preheat your grill to its highest setting. Grill the red peppers, turning as necessary, until the skins are blackened and blistered. Transfer to a bowl and cover tightly with cling film to seal – the trapped steam will help lift the skins and make the peppers much easier to peel.

Grill the chilli in the same way – it will char and blister much more quickly, so watch carefully. Add to the red peppers and re-cover the bowl.

Once cool, peel the skin off the red peppers and chilli, then cut open and discard the membrane and seeds.

Now, using a pestle and mortar, pound the pepper and chilli flesh with a good pinch of salt to a purée. Gradually add the extra virgin olive oil and stir well to combine. Taste and adjust the seasoning, adding a little more salt if necessary.

Potatoes with parsley, tarragon and olive oil

The combination of potatoes, tarragon and parsley is lovely with lobster. Serve at room temperature in a pretty bowl to pass around.

SERVES 4–6

1kg waxy potatoes

sea salt and freshly ground black pepper

small bunch of flat-leaf parsley, leaves only

small bunch of tarragon, leaves only

3 tbsp mild-tasting extra virgin olive oil

Place the potatoes in a saucepan, add enough cold water to just cover them and salt generously. Bring to the boil over a medium heat, turn the heat down and simmer until the potatoes feel tender right through when pierced with a knife; this will take 15–20 minutes.

Meanwhile, chop the parsley and tarragon leaves together.

Drain the potatoes and while still warm, dress with the extra virgin olive oil, salt and pepper. Stir in the chopped herbs.

Allow to cool slightly or to room temperature before serving.

Cucumber salad

This simple salad completes the meal perfectly. Both sharp and sweet, it is lovely with the potatoes as well as the lobster. Choose cucumbers that feel heavy for their size; their skin should be tight and vibrant in colour. (Illustrated on page 220.)

SERVES 4–6

2 medium cucumbers

bunch of dill, leaves only, finely chopped

3 tbsp good-quality white wine vinegar

2 tbsp caster sugar

sea salt and freshly ground black pepper

Peel the cucumbers, halve lengthways and scoop out the seeds. Slice as finely as you possibly can and then place the cucumber slices in a colander. Cover with a suitable-sized plate or saucer and place a heavy weight on top to press down. Set aside for an hour. The cucumbers will exude any excess moisture.

Transfer the cucumber slices to a bowl and sprinkle over the chopped dill. In a separate small bowl, whisk the wine vinegar and sugar together with some salt and pepper and pour over the cucumbers. Cover and leave to stand for 1–2 hours.

Taste the salad and adjust the seasoning as necessary, then pile into a shallow serving dish.

Soda bread

My friend Rory O'Connell, who happens to be one of my very favourite cooks, makes the best soda bread I have tasted. This recipe is from his sister, Darina Allen, and features in her book, Irish Traditional Cooking. Darina has kindly allowed me to include the recipe here, as it is a perfect match for this menu.

MAKES 1 LOAF

560g wholemeal flour

560g plain white flour, plus extra to dust

2 tsp salt

2 tsp bicarbonate of soda

750ml buttermilk

Preheat the oven to 230°C/Gas 8. Mix all the dry ingredients together in a large bowl. Make a well in the centre and add the buttermilk all at once. Working from the centre outwards, draw the flour into the liquid and mix to form a dough. It should be soft, but not too sticky.

Turn the dough out onto a well-floured surface and knead very lightly. Shape into a round, 5cm thick, and place on a baking sheet. Mark a deep cross on top of the dough. Bake in the oven for 20 minutes, then lower the oven setting to 200°C/Gas 6 and bake for a further 15 minutes. To test if it is cooked, tap the base gently – it should sound hollow.

Transfer the bread to a wire rack to cool. Soda bread should be eaten on the day it is made – preferably still warm from the oven, with butter.

Citrus tart

This sharp, tangy flavour of this tart filling is the perfect contrast to the rich, buttery pastry. It's a lovely way to finish a celebratory meal and you can make it in advance.

SERVES 8

Pastry

250g plain white flour, plus extra to dust

140g chilled unsalted butter, cut into cubes

1 tbsp caster sugar

½ tsp vanilla extract

1 organic free-range medium egg yolk

a little iced water

Filling

finely grated zest and juice of 5 oranges

juice of 2 lemons

300g caster sugar

5 organic free-range medium eggs

9 organic free-range medium egg yolks

300g unsalted butter, cut into cubes

To make the pastry, tip the flour into a food processor and add the chilled butter, sugar and vanilla extract. Pulse until you have the consistency of coarse breadcrumbs. Add the egg yolk and 1 tbsp iced water and pulse again; the pastry should begin to come together. Add a little more iced water as necessary, pulsing until the pastry forms a ball. (Be careful not to add too much water, as wet dough is difficult to work with.) Wrap in baking parchment or cling film and rest in the fridge for 30 minutes.

To make the filling, put all the ingredients, except the butter, into a large heavy-based pan. Whisk over the lowest possible heat (using a heat-diffuser mat if possible) until the sugar has dissolved; don't let the mixture overheat or it will curdle.

Add half the butter and continue to whisk until the mixture begins to thicken – it should coat the back of the spoon. Add the remaining butter and continue stirring until the mixture has become very thick; this will take about 10 minutes. Remove from the heat and pour into a cold bowl to halt the cooking process. The mixture will continue to thicken as it cools.

Roll out the pastry on a floured surface to a large round, about 3mm thick. Carefully lift the dough onto the rolling pin and drape it over a 25cm fluted flan tin, about 3cm deep. Press the pastry gently into the fluted sides and prick the base with a fork. Return to the fridge to chill for a further 30 minutes.

Preheat the oven to 180°C/Gas 4. Line the pastry case with greaseproof paper and baking beans (or dried beans) and bake 'blind' on the middle shelf of the oven for 20 minutes. Remove the paper and beans and return to the oven for a further 10 minutes until the base is dry. Remove from the oven and spoon the filling into the pastry case. Turn the oven setting up to 220°C/Gas 7 and return the tart to the oven. Cook for 8 minutes, or until the top has browned slightly.

Place the flan tin on a wire rack and leave the tart to cool. Serve in slices, with crème fraîche.

Time to spare

Some of my favourite cooking of all is done when there is time to spare – when the kitchen is quiet and I can make the things that please me most. Preserving different fruits in various ways during their precious short seasons has always appealed to me – so I can enjoy them throughout the year. I love the sight of glistening rows of jam and brandied fruits – like jewels – upon a shelf; they remind me of the seasons in which they were made. Often I find myself making far too many as I struggle to let go of the fruits I treasure most before they vanish for another year.

And there is the anticipatory excitement of cooking in advance for Christmas. A month or two ahead of the festive season, I'll prepare the puddings, knowing the mellowness of time will transform them into something magnificent to eat. More often than not, food that I prepare when I have time to myself is intended for others – a small gift of home-made jam or preserved fruit, perhaps, that can be treasured for more than just one day.

Vin de pêche

This is a delicious apéritif – the perfect drink for a balmy summer's evening. It takes only a few minutes to make; however you will need access to a peach tree, for it is the leaves that are used. Peach leaves taste of almonds when used in cooking, which is not so surprising as the trees are related. The best time to pick them is in the early summer when the leaves are still young and tender.

MAKES ABOUT 1 LITRE

60–80 peach leaves, freshly picked

1 bottle (750ml) light fruity red wine

500g caster sugar

125ml Cognac

Wash the peach leaves and pat dry with a clean tea towel. Place in a non-reactive container, such as a glass dish with a sealable lid, and add the wine, sugar and Cognac. Stir together well. Cover tightly and store in the fridge or a very cool dark place for around 15 days.

Strain the liquor through a fine sieve to remove the peach leaves and store in a sterilised bottle (see page 238) in the fridge.

Serve well chilled, over ice.

Strawberry and rhubarb cordial

I make cordials throughout the year using various fruits, including rhubarb, strawberries, raspberries, gooseberries, greengages, nectarines and peaches. They each have their own character and make a good alternative to wine, for those who would rather not be drinking alcohol. I make large jugfuls to place on the table – adding plenty of ice.

With this particular cordial, I'm always surprised that the gentle sweet flavour of the strawberries dominates the sharp intensity of the rhubarb. Make this cordial when English strawberries are in season – their flavour cannot be bettered.

MAKES ABOUT 800ML

8 medium rhubarb stalks

280g caster sugar

280ml water

300g strawberries, hulled and quartered

Wash and dry the rhubarb, then cut into 5cm lengths. Place in a heavy-based saucepan along with the sugar and water. Bring to the boil over a medium heat, stirring well to encourage the sugar to dissolve. Remove from the heat and add the strawberries.

Strain through a fine sieve into a jug, pressing firmly with the back of a small ladle to extract as much juice as possible. At first the syrup will appear quite thin, but as you press down and the fruit pulp passes through it will thicken. Pour into a sterilised bottle (see page 238) and leave to cool.

Once cooled, seal the bottle and store in the fridge. The cordial will keep for a month or so.

❀ Almost every fruit lends itself to making cordial. The method is always the same, though the sugar content will need adjusting and soft fruit really needs the addition of a little lemon juice.

❀ For a gooseberry cordial, use 400g gooseberries, 280g caster sugar, 1 litre water and 6 sprigs of lemon verbena, bruising these with a rolling pin before adding them to the pan with the other ingredients. Simmer and strain as above.

❀ Or, for a simple raspberry cordial, simmer 600g raspberries with 300g caster sugar, 1 litre water and the juice of ½ lemon for 6–7 minutes, then strain as above.

Raspberries preserved in brandy

Raspberries, greengages, figs and cherries will all sit happily in brandy for a year or so if kept in the fridge. We most often add brandied raspberries and cherries, in particular, to Prosecco to serve as an apéritif. They are also delicious eaten with bresaola and thinly sliced fennel as a first course, folded through vanilla ice cream, added to a trifle, scattered around a panna cotta, or served with biscotti and a little bitter chocolate.

Use just ripe fruit, without bruises or blemishes or soft spots. Adjust the sugar if you like, as the ideal amount will vary according to the sweetness of your chosen fruit. My favourite variety of raspberries is tulameen, which has a lovely mellow flavour and is around during late summer.

MAKE ABOUT 750ML

500g just ripe raspberries (or other chosen fruit)

7 tbsp caster sugar

3 tbsp water

200ml good-quality inexpensive brandy

Rinse the raspberries very gently; do not bother to pat them dry. Pack the fruit carefully into sterilised jars (see page 238).

Put the sugar and water into a saucepan and dissolve over a low heat, then add the brandy. Pour the sweetened brandy over the raspberries to cover them completely. Allow to cool, then seal and store in the fridge. Use within a year.

Spiced pears

I love the idea of sweet, spicy fruit with meat. One of my favourite things to eat is bollito misto – *an Italian assortment of poached meat – accompanied by salsa verde and mustard fruits. If you happen to have a pear tree in your garden, this recipe is one way to make good use of an autumnal glut. A bowl of these handsome-looking pears is particularly lovely alongside a baked ham (see page 201). You can also serve them with terrines, or use them in a winter fruit compote.*

Ideally, you want fruit that is just ripe or even slightly underripe; soft fruit is likely to disintegrate. I find the Comice and Conference varieties are the best to use here.

MAKES ABOUT 1KG

6 firm, ripe pears
(preferably Conference
or Comice)

Spiced syrup

300g caster sugar

200ml red wine vinegar

100ml water

1 cinnamon stick

5 cloves

small sprig of bay leaves
(optional)

First make the spiced syrup. Put the sugar, wine vinegar, water, spices and bay leaves if using into a saucepan and slowly bring to the boil, stirring once or twice to help dissolve the sugar. Let simmer for 5 minutes, then remove from the heat and leave to cool slightly.

Peel and halve the pears. Scoop out the cores if preferred (though this isn't essential if you don't mind serving the fruit with pips). Pack the pears into sterilised jars (see page 238), then pour the spiced syrup over them.

Seal and store in the fridge. Use within 3 months.

Damson jam

Damsons are a small variety of plum, in season from late August until the end of September. With their deep purple skins and contrasting pretty yellow flesh, they are one of the treats of early autumn. Sharp and sour in flavour, damsons are best cooked and used for a pie filling, creamy fool, ice cream or sorbet, or made into jam. High in pectin, they are particularly good for jam-making. This lovely sticky jam is perfect on warm scones, fresh from the oven, with unsalted butter.

MAKES ABOUT 1.2KG

1kg damsons

750g caster sugar

225ml water

Wash the damsons carefully and pat dry, rejecting any that are bruised or blemished. Cut in half and remove the stones.

Put the damsons and sugar into a preserving pan along with the water and place over a low heat. Cook gently for 15 minutes, stirring frequently until the sugar has dissolved, then turn up the heat and cook for a further 10–15 minutes until the fruit is tender and the skins are soft, removing any scum that rises to the surface during cooking with a small ladle.

Once the jam looks firm, test for setting (see page 240). As soon as it is ready, remove from the heat and spoon into warm sterilised jars (see below), filling them almost to the top. Cover the surface with a disc of waxed paper or baking parchment and allow to cool, then seal with a lid. If stored in a cool, dark place, this jam will keep for up to a year.

To sterilise jam jars or bottles, you can simply put them through the hot cycle in your dishwater. Alternatively, wash them in very hot water with a squeeze of washing-up liquid added, rinse thoroughly and dry in a warm oven.

Cherry jam with rose-scented geranium

The leaves of the rose-scented geranium are sweet smelling with an intense fragrance of roses. I have a healthy and vigorous plant in a pot in my garden, which I move into the kitchen when it turns cold. I infuse baked rice pudding, cherry cordial and the custard base for vanilla ice cream with the leaves. Here, they lend the jam a delicate scent that is somehow very feminine. Use plump, sweet, dark cherries that have a high proportion of flesh to stone.

MAKES ABOUT 1.2G

1kg dark, ripe,
sweet cherries

800g caster sugar

juice of 1 lemon

10 rose-scented
geranium leaves

Rinse the cherries carefully under cold running water, then drain well and pat dry with a clean cloth. Remove the stalks and stones, using a cherry stoner, and place in a large non-reactive (ceramic or glass) bowl along with the sugar, lemon juice and geranium leaves. Stir gently, then cover and leave to macerate for 1 hour.

Tip the contents of the bowl into a preserving pan and bring to a simmer, then remove from the heat and leave to cool to room temperature. Cover and leave in the fridge overnight.

The next day, tip the cherries into a fine sieve set over a bowl to catch the juice. Once the juice has drained through, pour it into a preserving pan and add the geranium leaves from the sieve; set the cherries aside.

Bring the juice to the boil and simmer, stirring, for 5 minutes, carefully skimming off any froth from the surface. Remove the geranium leaves with a slotted spoon and discard.

Now add the cherries to the syrup, return to the heat and boil for a further 5 minutes. Test for setting (see below).

Immediately spoon the jam into warm sterilised jars (see page 238), filling them almost to the top. Cover the surface with a disc of waxed paper or baking parchment. Allow to cool, then seal with a lid. Store in the fridge and use within 6 months.

To test for setting, put a saucer into the fridge to chill before you start to prepare the jam. Once the jam is cooked, it should set (on cooling) but it's always advisable to check. Put a teaspoonful of the jam onto the chilled saucer. Leave for a minute, then push with your finger – if the surface wrinkles and the jam appears to be setting it is ready. If not, return to the heat and cook for another minute or two, then test again.

Raspberry and nectarine jam

This is one of my favourite jams – sweet, chunky slices of nectarine or peach and raspberries in a sugar syrup with a hint of lemon. It's delicious on crusty sourdough or rye toast spread generously with unsalted butter.

MAKES ABOUT 1.8KG

1kg ripe nectarines or peaches

1kg raspberries (preferably home-grown)

1.6kg caster sugar

juice of 3 lemons

Bring a large saucepan of water to the boil. Using a small knife, mark a shallow cross in the base of each nectarine. Plunge the nectarines into the boiling water for 1 minute, then remove with a slotted spoon and refresh briefly in cool water. Once the fruit is cool enough to handle, peel away the skins, halve the nectarines and remove their stones. Cut each half into 4 or 5 slices.

Place the nectarines in a preserving pan with the raspberries, sugar and lemon juice. Slowly bring to a simmer, stirring to dissolve the sugar, then pour into a non-reactive bowl and allow to cool.

Cover the bowl of fruit with cling film and leave to stand in a cool place for at least 6 hours, or preferably overnight in the fridge.

Return the fruit mixture to the preserving pan. Bring to the boil, stirring gently, then cook rapidly for 10 minutes or until setting point is reached (test for setting, see left).

Immediately spoon the jam into warm sterilised jars (see page 238), filling them almost to the top. Cover the surface with a disc of waxed paper or baking parchment and allow to cool, then seal and store in the fridge. Use within 6 months.

Seville orange marmalade

Making marmalade has become something of a tradition in the month of February at Petersham.
Winter is the time for citrus fruit: oranges, lemons, kumquats, clementines and – for the making of
marmalade – small, bitter, pale-fleshed Seville oranges. Almost impossible to eat just as they are,
for their tartness is extreme, Seville oranges make the best marmalade of all – with a wonderful depth
of tangy flavour and a slight sharpness, which is needed. Make more than a couple of jars, as the
flavour will improve throughout the year, becoming slightly mellower and more complex.

MAKES ABOUT 2.5KG

1kg Seville oranges

3 litres water

2 pinches of salt

about 2kg caster sugar

Scrub the oranges clean, then finely slice the fruit into pinwheels, using a sharp knife, leaving on the skin but removing all pips and the central pithy membrane.

Put the fruit, water and salt into a large preserving pan and place over a medium heat. Bring to the boil, lower the heat and simmer gently until the peel is soft; this will take 1½–2 hours. Remove from the heat and leave to cool to room temperature. Transfer to a large ceramic or glass bowl, cover and leave to stand in a cool place for 24 hours.

The following day, measure the fruit and water into a clean preserving pan. Bring to the boil and for every cupful of the mixture, add a cupful of sugar. Bring back to the boil.

Cook steadily for 20 minutes or so until setting point is reached. To check, put a teaspoonful of the marmalade onto a chilled saucer. Leave for a minute, then push with your finger – if the surface wrinkles and the marmalade appears to be setting it is ready. Take off the heat and remove any scum from the surface with a skimming spoon.

Leave to stand for 5 minutes, then stir gently to distribute the fruit. Spoon into warm sterilised jars (see page 238), filling them almost to the top. Cover the surface with a disc of waxed paper or baking parchment and allow to cool, then seal and store in a cool, dark, dry place. Use the marmalade within 12 months.

Blackberry jelly

Beautifully glossy and black, this wobbly soft-set jelly is delicious paired with sheep's milk pecorino and walnuts or stronger creamy, goat's cheeses, such as St Tola from Ireland. I also dollop it on top of warm scones, fresh from the oven, and melt it to use as a glaze for brushing over fruit tarts. Growing in abundance in hedgerows, blackberries are food for free. Select plump, ripe berries and make your jelly soon after picking. As blackberries are low in pectin, an apple is added to help the setting.

MAKES 4–5 SMALL JARS

1.5kg blackberries

1 tart, crisp apple, such as Braeburn or Cox's

juice of 1 lemon

750g caster sugar

Rinse the blackberries and pick over them to remove any little stalks. Discard any blemished or mouldy fruit.

Place the berries in a large heavy-based non-reactive pan. Halve, core, peel and chop the apple, then add to the blackberries. Pour in enough water to give a 1cm depth, no more, and bring to a simmer. Cook gently over a medium heat for 10 minutes. Remove from the heat.

Tip the contents of the pan into a muslin-lined large sieve. To obtain the clearest possible jelly, let the juice drip through slowly on its own – it may well need to be left overnight to do so. If you are not concerned about the clarity or lack patience (or both), press the fruit, using the back of a ladle, to extract as much juice as possible. You should have about 1 litre.

Return the juice to the pan and add the lemon juice and sugar. Bring to the boil over a high heat, stirring until the sugar has dissolved. Now boil steadily, without stirring, for about 8–10 minutes until setting point is reached. As the jelly reduces, skim off any scum from the surface. To test for set, place a spoonful on a chilled plate – it should be the consistency of a thick syrup. Err on the loose side here, rather than risk a rubbery jelly.

Ladle the hot blackberry syrup into warm sterilised jars (see page 238), to 5mm from the rim. Cover the surface with discs of waxed paper or baking parchment to fit snugly on top of the jelly and leave to cool. Once cool, seal the jars and store in the fridge. The jelly should keep for up to a year.

Slow-roasted tomatoes

These tomatoes have a sweet, intense flavour. I add them to all kinds of dishes, including salads, vegetables, fish and scrambled eggs, and they are lovely with cheeses.

MAKES 1 MEDIUM JAR

6–8 ripe San Marzano or other plum tomatoes

10g caster sugar

10g sea salt

10g freshly ground black pepper

extra virgin olive oil

Preheat the oven to its lowest setting – probably 100°C/ Gas ¼. Halve the tomatoes lengthways and lay them, cut side up, in a single layer on a large baking tray. Mix together the sugar, salt and pepper, then sprinkle over the cut surface of the tomatoes. Roast in the oven, undisturbed, for 3–4 hours until they shrivel up. Remove and leave to cool.

Pack the tomatoes in sterilised jars (see page 238), cover with a layer of extra virgin olive oil, seal and store in the fridge. Use within a month.

Christmas pudding

I unashamedly adore Christmas pudding and I'm perplexed by those who say they don't. What could possibly be more tempting than a steaming pudding – irresistibly fragrant with a mix of spices, molasses sugar, candied peel, dried fruit and brandy – arriving at the table? These puddings will happily keep for a year in the fridge, their flavour becoming ever more delicious.

MAKES 2 PUDDINGS;
EACH SERVES 6

360g suet, grated

170g plain flour

180g fresh white
breadcrumbs

150g candied peel

350g seedless raisins

350g currants

200g sultanas

170g dark muscovado
sugar

grated zest of 1 lemon

grated zest of 1 orange

½ nutmeg, grated

½ tsp salt

½ tsp ground cinnamon

juice of ½ lemon

4 organic free-range
large eggs, lightly
beaten

100ml Armagnac

550ml whole milk

butter, to grease

To serve

small ladleful of brandy

Stir all the pudding ingredients together in a large mixing bowl until evenly combined; the mixture should feel quite wet. Cover the bowl with a clean cloth and leave to stand in a cool place overnight.

The following day pack the mixture firmly into two lightly greased 1 litre pudding basins. Cover the surface with a disc of baking parchment, then cover each basin with a double layer of parchment and secure under the rim with string. Place a trivet in each of two large saucepans (or cook the puddings one at a time). Stand the basin(s) on the trivet(s). Pour in enough boiling water to come two-thirds of the way up the side of the basin and put the lid on.

Bring to the boil over a high heat, then lower the heat slightly and cook for 6 hours, topping up the pan with boiling water as necessary. Lift out the pudding basin and leave the pudding to cool to room temperature. Re-cover with clean baking parchment and a layer of foil and place in the fridge or store in a cool, dry cupboard until needed.

On Christmas morning, boil the pudding (as above) for 1½–2 hours.

Warm the brandy just before serving. Turn out the pudding onto a warm plate, pour on the warm brandy and set alight. Bring the flaming pudding to the table. Serve brandy butter alongside, and perhaps a jug of thick pouring cream for those who prefer it.

Make your own brandy butter using just three ingredients: unsalted butter, icing sugar and Armagnac. The proportions don't really matter – it's the quality of the ingredients that counts. Allow 175g unsalted butter for 6 generous servings. Beat the butter until soft and creamy, then beat in about 150g icing sugar and 2–3 tbsp Armagnac to taste.

❀ To seal the Christmas pudding ready for steaming, cover with a generous double layer of baking parchment, pleating it in the centre as shown (this allows room for the pudding to expand during steaming). Tie securely in place with kitchen string, positioning it tightly around the basin just below the rim. Leave a length of string to act as a handle for lifting the basin out of the pan.

Index

Acknowledgements

I should like thank all staff at Petersham, past and present, without whom the restaurant would not exist. A special thanks to Ros Shiers and Emma Miller who worked alongside me in the kitchen on the photography shoots, helping to make them fun and inspiring.

Thank you to Jason Lowe, whose beautiful photographs once again grace the pages of this book; to Lawrence Morton and Cynthia Inions for the layout and styling – their work is second to none. A big thank you to my editor Janet Illsley, who has the patience to work with me. And to all those at Quadrille, especially Jane O'Shea who has given me the freedom to write another book that rings true for me.

Not forgetting my daughters, Holly and Evie, whose enthusiasm and fearlessness in the kitchen makes cooking that much more fun at home. And my friend Fiona, whose table I have sat at more times than I can remember and enjoyed some of the most memorable meals of my life.

And finally, this book is for Rose, whose great talent in the kitchen, generosity of spirit and indomitable nature is missed by so many.

Publishing director Jane O'Shea
Creative director Helen Lewis
Project editor Janet Illsley
Art direction & design Lawrence Morton
Photographer Jason Lowe
Props stylist Cynthia Inions
Production Marina Asenjo, Vincent Smith

First published in 2010 by
Quadrille Publishing Limited
Alhambra House,
27–31 Charing Cross
Road, London WC2H 0LS

www.quadrille.co.uk

Cataloguing in Publication Data: a catalogue record for
this book is available from the British Library.

ISBN 978 184400 850 6

Printed in China